THE FOLIO PHENOMENON

THE FOLIO PHENOMENON

New Freedom to Customize Your Investments and Increase Your Wealth

GENE WALDEN

Dearborn™
Trade Publishing
A **Kaplan Professional** Company

This publication is designed to provide accurate and authoritative information in regard to the subject matter covered. It is sold with the understanding that the publisher is not engaged in rendering legal, accounting, or other professional service. If legal advice or other expert assistance is required, the services of a competent professional person should be sought.

Editorial Director: Donald J. Hull
Senior Managing Editor: Jack Kiburz
Interior Design: Lucy Jenkins
Cover Design: Scott Rattray, Rattray Design
Typesetting: the dotted i

Library of Congress Cataloging-in-Publication Data

Walden, Gene.
   The folio phenomenon : new freedom to customize your investments and increase your wealth / Gene Walden.
      p.   cm.
   Includes index.
   ISBN 0-7931-5410-3
   1. Folios (Securities)—Handbooks, manuals, etc.   2. Portfolio management—Handbooks, manuals, etc.   I. Title.
   HG4529.5 .W35 2002
   332.63′27—dc21

                                                                2002001822

DEDICATION

To Dan, Shirley, David, Charles, Midget, Jimmy, James, Helen, Helen, Earl, and Earl, Sr.

CONTENTS

ACKNOWLEDGMENTS

A number of people have contributed to the success of this book. Don Hull, Dearborn Trade Publishing editorial director, helped me shape the book into a simple yet comprehensive guide that even small investors can use to command their own diverse portfolios. Larry Nelson, who has worked on most of my *100 Best Stocks* books, also contributed to this project, helping with the research and fact gathering. I also want to thank Jack Kiburz, senior managing editor at Dearborn Trade; Sandy Thomas, senior editorial assistant; and Cynthia Zigmund, vice president and publisher, for their help in putting this project into print.

CHAPTER 1

THE FOLIO PHENOMENON

A t last, there's a concept that puts the fun into stock market investing even for investors of the most modest means. No longer do you have to choose between Coke and Pepsi, Ford and GM, or Apple and IBM. You can own them all. Creating your own personal mutual fund has never been easier. You have the freedom to build the portfolio you've always wanted and to add to it or change it whenever you wish.

Thanks to an ingenious new investment service known as Folios (or "stock baskets"), individual investors can play in the same league as professional money managers—buying, selling, and adding to their positions easily and economically.

Limited assets and high brokerage commissions are no longer an obstacle to small investors who want to build a well-diversified portfolio that they can actively manage.

Folios are the next big thing in the investment world—and the best thing to come along for individual investors since the advent of the mutual fund. In fact, for many investors, Folios represent a dramatic improvement over mutual funds as well as traditional commission-based stock trading. In a nutshell, Folios provide the diversification benefits of mutual funds with the control and tax efficiency of direct stock ownership.

Consider this: You can build a portfolio of 50 stocks and actively manage it, buying, selling, and adding to your positions regularly for under $150 per year flat fee! At a traditional brokerage house, that same $150 would buy you, at most, two trades. Or to look at it another way, if you choose the $14.95 monthly Folio payment option, you will get up to 500 free trades per month. Even at most online discount brokers such as E*Trade, $14.95 would only afford you one trade. In other words, Folios can get you 500 trades for the price of one.

That's why Folios are creating not just a ripple but a revolution across the entire brokerage industry. Born of the convergence of the Internet and advanced software technology and computer processing power, Folios are changing the investing game forever. For the first time ever, it's as cheap and easy to invest in large groups of stocks through dollar cost averaging as it is to buy no-load mutual funds.

"For someone who wants to build and manage their own portfolio, it's a very cheap option," says Dr. John Markese, president of the American Association of Individual Investors (AAII). Folios give investors—even those with relatively modest means—the ability to invest in a large group of stocks and trade within their portfolio on a regular basis without incurring the high commission costs formally associated with buying and selling stocks. "It's hard to see any disadvantages for long-term investors who want to build their own portfolio," adds Markese.

How is it possible to trade stocks so inexpensively? Folio companies use a process known as "window trades" to save on transaction costs. Customers submit orders throughout the day, and the Folio firm holds onto those orders until it can make all its trades in bulk. Most Folio operations make window trades two or three times a day—at least once in the morning and once in the afternoon. For investors, it means they won't get instant execution of their orders, but trades are made the same day—and at tremendous savings.

SHAKING UP THE INDUSTRY

The Folio concept is such an attractive option that some other players within the brokerage industry have done their best to try to stop it and put Folios out of business. The Investment Company Institute, an advocacy organization for the mutual fund industry, filed a petition with the U.S. Securities and Exchange Commission (SEC) requesting that Folios be regulated as mutual funds. The SEC denied the request.

"Their motivation was solely to slow us down, stop us, do anything they could to have this concept not occur," claims Steve Wallman, founder and CEO of FOLIO*fn*, a leading Folio company. "I think they quite mistakenly thought that what we were doing was completely competitive with the mutual fund industry. But it's not. We view Folios as an alternative—a superior alternative—to the traditional mutual fund, but not a replacement."

The major distinction between Folios and funds, says Wallman, is that funds are actively managed by a professional money manager, while Folios are managed by individual investors. The SEC's decision not to classify Folios as funds eliminated a lot of red tape the Folio industry would otherwise have faced. "We would have been subjected to a whole series of rules that may have made it impossible to offer Folios, which is what the mutual fund industry was really hoping for," explains Wallman. "For example, a mutual fund has to have an independent board of directors for the fund. That makes sense if you have a fund, but a Folio isn't a fund, it's just a list of stocks. Does that mean that each separate account somebody sets up has to have a board of directors? If you set up a Folio, should you have to have an independent board of directors for your own account? That just doesn't make sense."

The mutual fund industry is not the only group concerned about the emergence of the Folio concept. Brokerage companies—both traditional full-service brokers and discounters—are keeping a wary eye on the Folio industry. In fact, some of the leading online brokers, including E*Trade and Fidelity, have already launched their own stock basket offerings, although their service falls short of some of the other Folio-related companies. More brokers are sure to follow suit.

"The securities end of the business actually likes what we're doing," says Wallman. "It gives them a new service they can offer. I think traditional brokers will be using Folios more and more. We're already offering our Folios through Quick & Reilly, and we're talking to some of the larger wire houses about using our platform internally to deliver Folios to their customers. In fact, a couple full-service brokers want to use us internally as a means to create model portfolios that would be available to sell through their registered reps around the country."

Eventually, adds Wallman, full-service brokers will use Folios as a value-added service for many of their customers. "I think they'll come out with their preferred list of maybe 30 stocks, and they'll say 'Here is a portfolio of the 30 stocks that we recommend at this point.' They'll be able to do that instead of what they have been doing, which is recommending stocks one at a time. Now you can buy a whole bunch of shares instead of one stock or two or three. The problem with that is that frequently one or two of those stocks will go down, which causes the broker to lose customers. That's a very risky way to invest. With Folios, brokers can say 'Our research department has come up with 30 stocks it recommends, and we can put you into all of those stocks with one push of the button.' That's a big improvement. That's why I see Folios generally as complementary and additive to both mutual funds and traditional brokerage services."

The purpose of this book is to introduce and explain the Folio concept and then to delve deeper into Folios. Chapters 4 and 5 will suggest Folios that you can use in your own investment portfolio as well as Folios from FOLIO*fn*, a leading player in the Folio business.

WHY FOLIOS? THE PROS AND CONS

Low transaction costs are just one of many advantages Folio investing offers over traditional brokers and mutual funds. Here are several others.

Limited Resources; Big Portfolio

One of the biggest advantages of Folio-type accounts is that they give investors of modest means the ability to own a vast portfolio of stocks. Under the traditional brokerage system, building a diversified portfolio was typically a long and fairly expensive proposition. If you didn't have at least $50,000 to $100,000 to throw at the market, it was hard to put together a truly diversified portfolio.

For instance, an investor starting with $10,000 would find it very inefficient to buy more than a few stocks. To build a portfolio of 40 different stocks, the investor could buy, on average, only about $250 of each stock—minus commissions. And commissions at full-service brokerages run about $75 to $100 per trade, which means that about a third of your investment dollars would go to commissions. Even with online discount brokers, which typically charge only about $15 per trade, commission costs would come to about $600 for 40 stock purchases. And that's just to get the portfolio started. If you wanted to add to it regularly—perhaps $1,000 a month—it simply wouldn't be practical to spread your contribution evenly throughout the entire portfolio.

With Folios, not only are you able to open the account with a full portfolio of stocks of your choosing, you can also add to it a little at a time without incurring additional commissions. (Some will charge a very small fee.) In fact, some Folio programs allow you to spread your investment dollars evenly throughout the portfolio—even if it means buying fractional shares of many of the stocks on your list.

Buy in Dollars, Not Shares

Folios give investors the option of buying or selling stocks based on a set dollar amount rather than a specific number of shares. For instance, if you want to invest $300 per month across your entire portfolio, you can do that with Folio investing. Or you can make changes—small or large—in the balance of your portfolio at any time. In other words, if you want to increase the percentage of your holdings in ten of your favorite stocks and reduce the percentage of several others, you can do that with a single order. Although policies can vary, with some Folio programs you can buy or sell stocks in any quantity at any time at no additional charge.

As the chart demonstrates, for all but the smallest traders, investing through Folios is much cheaper than investing through either a full-service broker or a discounter. (However, the level of service also varies.)

Folios versus Other Brokers: Cost Comparison

Trades per Year	Full-Service Broker	Regular Discount Broker	Online Discounter	Folio Investing
1	$ 80*	$ 40†	$ 15‡	$150§
5	400	200	75	150
10	800	400	150	150
20	1,600	800	300	150
50	4,000	2,000	750	150
100	8,000	4,000	1,500	150
500	40,000	20,000	7,500	150
1,000	80,000	40,000	15,000	150

*Assumes the full-service firm charges about $80 per trade for smaller trades.
†Assumes the discount firm charges about $40 per trade for small trades.
‡Assumes a charge of about $15 per trade, which is about average for online discount brokers.
§The annual flat fee charged by leading folio companies is about $150.

Pick Your Own or Buy a Basket (or Buy a Basket and Change It)

You can choose any stocks you want for your portfolio, drawing on your own research and investment objectives. Or you can invest in any of dozens of preselected baskets of stocks.

If you prefer picking stocks yourself, you could enjoy hours of fun sorting through stock research data and selecting a full portfolio of stocks that best suit your investment objectives. (Chapter 3 offers a detailed plan for selecting your own all-star portfolio.) Or pick two or three different portfolios. One company gives you the option of owning up to three 50-stock portfolios for $295 a year.

Investors who are not confident picking their own stocks can find plenty of preselected Folios from which to choose. Some Folio companies offer preselected Folios that match a certain sector or cover a broad cross-section of the market. FOLIO*fn* offers the widest selection of Folios, with about 150 different ones, including growth stock portfolios, sector stock Folios, ethical stock Folios, and a wide range of other specialty Folios. (Many of those Folios are listed in Chapter 5.)

You could also choose your portfolio from a market index, such as the Dow Jones Industrial Average.

Or you can use this book to pick your portfolios. I've included several portfolio suggestions in Chapter 4 (also listed at AllstarStocks.com.), including blue chips, small stocks, tech stocks, high yielding stocks, and growth and income stocks.

Even if you choose a preselected Folio from this book or from a Folio company, you are not obliged to hold those exact stocks. Adjusting the list to your liking—by selling some stocks on the list, adding more stocks, or replacing some stocks with others of your choosing—is all part of the Folio service. Some investors may change their portfolios several times a month. It's your money and your Folio, and you can do with it whatever you wish in order to make the Folio work best for you.

Once you've selected a portfolio, you also can change the weighting of your holdings with a single keystroke. A preselected Folio may have 25 stocks with equal weighting (in other words, each of the 25 stocks would account for 4 percent of the overall portfolio). You may decide that you want a heavier weighting of a few of your favorite stocks on the list, with less emphasis on the rest of the stocks. In short, you have full control over every aspect of the portfolio—and all for a modest monthly or annual fee.

"If you decide to buy a Dow Jones Industrial Average Folio," says FOLIO*fn*'s Wallman, "you can customize it as you want. You don't have to have Philip Morris in it if you don't like tobacco stocks. You can overweight Microsoft if you think that it's going to be a better place for the future. You're in a position to harvest tax losses out of it and do other things that are better than what you can get through a mutual fund or index fund."

Investment Clubs Can Play, Too

Thanks to an agreement between one of the leading Folio firms and the National Association of Investment Clubs (NAIC), investment clubs can also participate in Folio investing. ICLUBcentral.com is the online presence for about 45,000 investment clubs that are registered through the NAIC. Through its agreement with FOLIO*fn*, clubs will be able to create and manage their own Folios and make hundreds of trades each month at no additional charge aside from the standard annual or monthly fee. Club members also can log on any time to monitor the performance of their club account.

Several hundred credit unions also have begun offering Folios for their members, and more credit unions are joining every month. Under the arrangement, credit union members can invest in Folios for a flat standard fee.

Brokers Also Are Joining

A growing legion of brokerage companies and financial planners also has begun joining the Folio movement. Customers of some investment firms can buy portfolios of stocks through their broker at a flat monthly or annual fee. For those investors who like the Folio concept but need some outside investment guidance, the Folios now can offer the best of both worlds. Their brokers can help them set up a large portfolio of stocks and offer advice along the way regarding adjustments to their portfolio for a flat annual or monthly fee.

FOLIOS VERSUS MUTUAL FUNDS

For the independent investor, Folio investing has some decided advantages over mutual funds. But for those who aren't turned on by earnings reports, stock tables, price-earnings ratios, and the day-to-day dilemma of whether to buy, hold, or sell, mutual funds are probably the proper choice.

Funds offer instant diversification and professional management, all for a relatively small fee. They give you a chance to own a broad portfolio of stocks without concerning yourself with the vast complexities of the daily market. What could be simpler? Buy some good funds, add to them regularly through dollar cost averaging, and move on with your life. Let the fund managers sweat the details.

But for investors who enjoy doing their own research and making their own buy-and-sell decisions, investing in a Folio of stocks would have some significant advantages over mutual funds. In addition to control and tax advantages, you can buy stocks in smaller lots, enabling you to get in and out of a stock faster. You can own a smaller group of stocks rather than the dozens or hundreds of different stocks many mutual funds own, and you have more control over the flow of money into the portfolio. You also can focus on the long term, unlike mutual fund managers who see their daily and yearly performance figures printed in the newspaper every day.

Folios will probably not replace mutual funds, but Wallman thinks they will certainly cut into the mutual fund market. "As Folios become more and more pervasive, you'd have to ask why anybody would keep buying mutual funds. Clearly, the traditional mutual fund is not as good a vehicle for investing as Folios because of the tax benefits, the customization benefits, the cost control benefits, and other advantages of Folios."

Wallman concedes, however, that there will probably always be investors who prefer funds. "If you don't care what you own, you're a passive investor, and you want to own the stocks of an index, such as the Dow Jones Industrial Average or the S&P 500, you might as well stick with funds."

Adds John Markese of the AAII, "Folios will be an important player in the investment market, but they won't eliminate mutual funds."

Here are some of the key advantages Folios have over mutual funds.

More Control Over What You Own

Folios provide the broad diversification of a mutual fund, but you decide which stocks to own and which ones to sell. It's very much like operating your own mutual fund. Although the brunt of the research and stock selection process is on your shoulders, the benefit is that you know what you own, why you bought it, and what you paid for it. And you decide when—if ever—to sell a stock. There are no stocks in your portfolio that you don't like, and no companies from industries you don't endorse. And you determine the precise mix of stocks in your portfolio.

You decide—based on your own threshold for risk—exactly how diversified or specialized your portfolio should be, guiding your investment decisions based on your own unique investment philosophy.

You Control the Taxes

Mutual fund investors have no control over the buying and selling of stocks within a fund, which means they have no control over the taxable gains and losses that come from the sale of stocks within the fund's portfolio. Even if you hold a fund for the long term, you are subject to taxes on the gains from stock sales within the fund. That means that every time a fund manager sells a stock for a gain within the fund, you could be subject to taxes on that gain.

But with Folio investing, you have full control over the tax management. You can manage your buying and selling to minimize taxable gains. Or you can hold your stocks for the long term and pay no taxes. With stocks, you pay no taxes on the gains until you sell the stock. So you could own a stock that grows 100-fold and still pay no taxes on those gains as long as you hold the stock.

A tax gain and loss tracking system at some Folio Web sites makes it even easier to trade stocks efficiently. "Every gain and every loss is detailed by stock, which makes it easier to balance them out for your own tax purposes," says Steve Cohen, FOLIO*fn* vice president of marketing.

Percentage Fees versus Fixed Fees

The fee structure for Folios is entirely different than that of mutual funds—often to the advantage of Folio investors. Many mutual funds charge an up-front fee known as a load that can amount to as much as 5 percent to 8 percent of your investment. And all mutual funds charge an annual fee to cover their expenses.

Annual expense fees for mutual funds generally vary from about 1 percent to 2.5 percent of the total amount invested in the fund. For small investors, the mutual fund fee structure might be preferable to the flat fee charged by some Folio operations. But the larger your investment, the greater the advantage Folios offer over mutual funds. The following chart compares the cost of mutual funds versus Folios for various levels of investment.

Folios versus Mutual Funds: Cost Comparison

Amount Invested	Charges	Load Mutual Fund	No-Load Fund	Folio
$ 5,000	Purchase fee	$ 250*	$ 0	$ 0
	Annual fee	75†	75†	150‡
10,000	Purchase fee	500	0	0
	Annual fee	150	150	150
25,000	Purchase fee	1,250	0	0
	Annual fee	375	375	150
50,000	Purchase fee	2,500	0	0
	Annual fee	750	750	150
100,000	Purchase fee	5,000	0	0
	Annual fee	1,500	1,500	150
500,000	Purchase fee	25,000	0	0
	Annual fee	7,500	7,500	150
1,000,000	Purchase fee	50,000	0	0
	Annual fee	15,000	15,000	150

*Assumes the fund charges a load of 5 percent, which is about average among all load mutual funds.
†Assumes the fund charges an annual fee of 1.5 percent, which is about average among all funds.
‡The amount charged by leading Folio companies is about $150 per year.

As the chart demonstrates, the bigger your investment, the greater the advantages Folios provide over mutual funds. For an investor starting out with just $5,000, clearly a no-load mutual fund is the more economical option. But a load fund with a 5 percent fee would actually cost you more than a Folio, even with a very modest $5,000 investment.

And as your investment portfolio grows, the Folio option becomes much more attractive. With a $100,000 investment, a typical load fund would cost about $5,000 up front and about $1,500 per year. Even a no-load fund would cost about $1,500 a year—which is about ten times the $150 annual fixed rate you would pay with a Folio. With even higher amounts, the difference becomes even more dramatic. A $1 million investment would cost about $50,000 up front for a typical load fund, plus an annual expense fee of about $15,000 per year A no-load fund would also run about $15,000 a year, while the flat-fee Folio would stay at just $150.

So for all but the most modest investors, the Folio option clearly offers some economical advantages.

THE DOWNSIDE TO FOLIOS

For all the advantages Folios offer, they are not ideal for every investor. Here are some drawbacks to Folios.

You Do the Research

Folios are geared to the do-it-yourself investor. Investors must make all the buying and selling decisions on their own. That means hours of work researching dozens of stocks to come up with the perfect ones for the portfolio. The Folio investor also must decide what to sell and when to sell it. Investors who have no interest or inclination in doing all of their own research and buying and selling of securities decide against opening a Folio account. A better choice might be to own mutual funds or to use a full-service broker or financial planner to help in the stock selection process.

However, if you already enjoy making your own decisions in the stock selection process, Folios could be the right investment for you. Some full-service brokerages are also beginning to offer accounts similar to Folios, with a couple of twists. You pay more, but you get the help of a full-service broker to set up and monitor your portfolio.

More Expensive for Small Investors

Different Folio companies offer different plans, but the plans offered by leading Folio companies may cost more than small investors would pay elsewhere. As mentioned earlier, for investors with less than $5,000 to invest, no-load mutual funds would be slightly cheaper than the leading Folio company (although some Folio companies have different cost structures that could favor smaller investors). The same would be true for small investors of individual stocks, who may make only a handful of trades per year.

Slightly More Expensive for Many Buy-and-Hold Investors

If you make fewer than ten stock trades per year, a fixed-rate Folio account may not be right for you (although a different type of Folio account could work). A typical transaction at an online brokerage company costs about $10 to $20. At $15 per trade, you could make about ten trades per year for about the same cost as the leading Folio company charges as an annual fee. One of the biggest advantages of the Folio concept is that it gives investors the opportunity to buy a broad portfolio of stocks and make numerous trades without worrying about commission costs. For investors itching to trade regularly, Folios are ideal.

If you're content to buy and hold for the long term, making occasional trades along the way, you might find the fixed-rate Folio plan more expensive. However, there are other Folio-type plans that are more economical for infrequent traders. For instance, one company charges $6.99 per month to hold an account—including up to two free trades per month and just $2.99 per trade thereafter. Even infrequent traders might find that type of account preferable to the traditional brokerage commission model.

And consider one more factor: If you want to dollar-cost-average in one stock just once a month, Folios are still cheaper than typical online discount brokers. Twelve $15 trades a year comes to $180—that's $31 more than the annual fee for a Folio company.

Trading Restrictions

Day traders are not likely to line up for Folio accounts, because the commission-free Folio trades are only executed about twice a day. Day traders buy and sell their stocks several times a day to take advantage of small vacillations in the market. However, Folio firms like FOLIO*fn* make trades in large batches known as "window trades" to keep costs down, which makes it possible to offer unlimited trades at such a low cost. FOLIO*fn* makes all its trades at 10:15 AM and 2:45 PM—with no trades executed in between unless you're willing to pay an extra $15 per trade. That arrangement simply wouldn't work for day traders or for other investors who like to buy a stock when it hits a specific price— either through a market order or a limit order.

"We're not right for day traders," says FOLIO*fn*'s Wallman. "Day trading is a different concept of how to play the market, but it has nothing to do with investing. That's not the market we're interested in. We're not pretending to offer streaming quotes from multiple market makers."

But for most long-term investors, the commission savings offered through window trades more than compensates for the restrictions on the timeliness of the trades. "There's a different kind of very active trader who is suitable for our system," adds Wallman. "They're not doing a lot of trades where they're trying to time the market moment by moment, but they're very active because they're buying 20, 30, or 40 stocks in a whole sector. They're moving from one sector to another— perhaps from 20 Internet stocks to 20 biotech stocks that they think are important. These people are very well suited for our system, because our system allows them to buy 20, 30, or 40 stocks all at once and do it on a very cost-effective basis, very efficiently, and with lots of tools to give them sector analysis, screening, and ready-to-go sector Folios."

Limited Selection of Commission-Free Stocks

Investors are limited in the selection of stocks they can buy commission-free through most Folio companies. Most offer free trades for about 4,000 of the most widely traded stocks in the U.S. market. And while that includes virtually all the blue chip and large capitalization stocks on the market, many smaller or newer stocks are excluded. An investor interested in building a portfolio of up-and-coming small stocks would have to pay extra fees to buy and sell some of those stocks. But that is rarely a problem, according to Wallman, who says that the available window stocks at FOLIO*fn* represent about 95 percent of the stock market's total capitalization and about 95 percent of all the trades in the market. And that selection continues to grow.

Despite its few limitations, the advantages of Folio investing for do-it-yourself investors greatly outweigh the disadvantages.

CHAPTER 2

RATING THE PLAYERS

The Folio field is growing, but by no means is it over-crowded yet. There are only a handful of real players in the stock basket business, along with a few other companies that offer something vaguely similar to the Folio concept. In this section, we'll take a close look at the services and fees of the leading players in the Folio-related market.

Although the Folio concept in its online form is brand new, some full-service brokerage companies have offered a slightly different all-you-can-trade option for their customers for several years. "Bits and pieces of the Folio concept have already been out there in the market," explains John Markese of the AAII. "Full-service brokers have offered wrap accounts that allow you to trade as much as you want for a certain percentage of your invested assets."

But those wrap accounts are still a far cry from the $150 annual flat fee of the online Folio companies. Most brokerage wrap accounts charge about 1½ percent to 2 percent of invested assets (with a minimum fee of about $1,500). For instance, if you have $100,000 in your account, you will pay about a 2 percent annual fee, which comes to $2,000 a year. Investors with over $1 million face a reduced percentage—about 1½ percent—which still comes to about $15,000 on a $1 million account. Is it worth it? Probably not for all but the most active traders.

That's why the much cheaper Folio concept is starting to sweep the investment industry.

There are four leading players in the Folio-related business—all with their own unique strengths and weaknesses. The company with the most to offer is FOLIO*fn*, which features more than 100 preselected Folios and an annual fee of as low as $149. Other leaders in the stock basket market include BuyandHold.com, which was the first to offer dollar-based investing and fractional share purchases for stocks on all the major exchanges (but does not offer preselected Folios); ShareBuilder.com, which offers customers a flat fee service for all stock purchases but charges $14.99 for all stock sales; and E*Trade, which offers basket trading for an annual percentage fee tied to the customer's total invested assets.

One other leading Folio company, NetFolio.com, became an early victim of the drawn-out bear market. The company folded in October 2001 after only seven months of operation. In a bad market, even the best innovations can be a difficult sell. "The slow economy in which they were operating was very difficult," says Steve Wallman, who launched FOLIO*fn* in September 2000, several months ahead of NetFolio. He believes timing was one of several factors that hurt NetFolio. "NetFolio started after us, they priced their product more expensively than ours, they weren't able to offer as good a product as we offer, and they just couldn't make it. It takes a long time to get something going like this that requires people's trust."

There may be other casualties to come in the Folio market—particularly if the big houses on Wall Street move into the market aggressively, according to Markese. "I think if Fidelity or Charles Schwab goes after this full force, they could take over the industry."

But Wallman contends that breaking into the flat fee Folio market will not be as easy as it looks. "The concept of charging a low flat fee each year is obviously easy. Anybody can do that. But the idea of making it work is actually very, very tough. The technology that underlies the ability to do portfolios cost-effectively so that you can offer them for a yearly $150 is extraordinarily complex. We have invested close to $100 million in this company, and a lot of that has been in system design and system build-out. We have had about 200 man-years of IT (information technology) work in the company. It is not an insignificant task. That's why Quick & Reilly wants to work with us, because they like getting the benefits of the system without investing all the money. E*Trade has a system similar to ours, but it took them 18 months to build, and they're nowhere close to where we are. That gives you a sense of how difficult and expensive this is to do."

Wallman founded FOLIO*fn* after serving as a commissioner on the U.S. Securities and Exchange Commission from 1994 to 1997. Prior to that he was a partner in the Washington, D.C. law firm Covington & Burling. Wallman came up with the Folio concept after studying the advances in computer technology and the Internet. "The main transformation for this concept came from two areas, having the computer power to process large scale transactions and the advent of the Internet where people, for the first time, could really have inexpensive, interactive two-way broadband communications," explains Wallman. "You need the confluence of both of those in order for it to work. If you had tried to do this ten years ago, you simply, technically, would not have been able to deliver."

Because of its technology, FOLIO*fn* can do millions of trades automatically through its computer system without any human interaction. "We can deliver these services at prices no one has ever see before," says Wallman. "It's something we're able to do, quite literally, because of the technology behind it."

FOLIO*fn* offers customers several pricing plans. For one portfolio of 50 stocks, you can pay $14.95 a month or $149 a year. For three portfolios of up to 50 stocks, the fee is $29.95 a month or $295 a year. For additional portfolios, the cost is $95 a year. The flat fee gives you the ability to make 500 free trades per month. All trades after that are $1. Window trades are made twice a day. Real time (market) trades cost $14.95 per trade.

The company offers well over 100 preselected portfolios from which to choose, or you can build your own portfolio or start with one of the preselected Folios and change it to your own tastes.

For investors who need a little help setting up their own portfolio, the FOLIO*fn* Web site has an interactive "wizard" that leads you through several questions to determine your investment goals and threshold for risk. Once you've completed the questionnaire, the wizard creates an investor profile, suggests an asset mix, and recommends three Folio choices per asset class.

The system gives investors total control of their portfolios. Even if you choose a preselected folio, you can balance your holdings however you wish. "You can assign weighting on each stock," says Steve Cohen of FOLIO*fn*. "Or you can automatically allocate your assets equally by dollar amount or proportionally based on each stock's market capitalization."

The FOLIO*fn* system also tracks every trade you make by tax lot and shows you tax gains or losses on each stock in your portfolio, making it easy to harvest your tax losses or manage your trades to minimize your tax gains. Another feature, vital stats, shows the performance of your folio, compares it with the major indexes, and breaks it down by other financial criteria.

The site also offers detailed stock research, including access to Zacks Investment Research and free quarterly sector reports from Argus Research. Another plus are the helpful articles on investing and timely columns to help investors manage their Folios.

FUTURE OFFERINGS

Wallman sees several improvements ahead for FOLIO*fn,* both in services and execution of trades. "As trading costs get lower and lower, we may be able to deliver real-time portfolio trading. We already offer something called "windows on demand" for very large institutions that want to make large trades. We make those window trades in real time."

Managed Folios are also on the horizon, according to Wallman. "There are three general customers in financial services. First are the do-it-yourselfers who use the discount brokers. Second are the delegators who delegate the management of their accounts to someone else. These range from people of high net worth to people who have their own private money manager or broker to people who use mutual funds. And third is the in-between group, or the "advised" investors. These are folks who don't want to make all the decisions on their own but want to be involved in the decision-making process.

"Our system actually works for all three types," adds Wallman. "Right now, it works for the do-it-yourselfer, but we will soon be offering managed Folios in which a manager makes the decisions on your Folio. We also will offer something for the third group, the advised investors. Under that system, the manager will place an order in your account and then send you an e-mail that says, in effect, your manager has suggested a change to your account. But it's up to you to decide if you want to accept it or not. You have the final say in the trading."

Under the new managed Folio technology, mutual fund managers would be able to set up stock portfolios at FOLIO*fn* that trade in tandem with their fund portfolios. "But instead of selling it as a fund, they can offer it to investors as an individual stock account with all the advantages that stock ownership provides," explains FOLIO*fn*'s Cohen. "A portfolio manager from American Century Funds or Aim Funds or any fund family can set up a portfolio at our site, and as they adjust their portfolio model, the system automatically changes it for all the accounts that own that portfolio."

The system, which the company dubs "synchronization," will allow investors to invest in managed model portfolios. "When the investment manager changes the model—maybe he or she wants to add more Microsoft shares—when he or she pushes the button, all the accounts subscribed to his or her model change," explains Wallman. "So now you have a separate managed account that is able to follow this actively managed model. You get all of the benefits of an actively managed mutual fund and none of the disadvantages, because you own each of the stocks in the portfolio. When someone else decides to sell his or her portfolio, it has no impact whatsoever on your portfolio or the taxes you have to pay."

One more feature that adds to the Folio allure is the exclusions option. If there are stocks you don't want, such as tobacco, nuclear power, or military stocks, you can indicate that in your account, and those stocks will be excluded from your managed portfolio. "You also can add your own picks," says Wallman. "Maybe you like the portfolio, but you have a few favorite stocks you'd like to add to the mix. That's something else you can do with Folios that you can't do with mutual funds."

FOLIO*fn* AT A GLANCE

Fees

FOLIO*fn* offers several fee options:

- *Monthly or yearly subscription fee.* For just $14.95 a month or $149 a year, you can have one Folio of up to 50 stocks and make up to 500 window trades per month. Additional trades over your first 500 are just $1 per trade. For three portfolios of up to 50 stocks, the fee is $29.95 a month or $295 a year. For additional portfolios, the cost is $95 a year. You also can have money from your bank or other account automatically invested in stocks for free.

- *Real-time transactions.* If you want to buy and sell stocks at the current market price, you pay a fee of $14.95 per transaction, which is similar to other online brokers.

- *Window trades are made two times a day.* The company offers window trades on about 4,000 stocks.

Investment Assistance

FOLIO*fn* offers the following investment assistance:

- *On-site research.* FOLIO*fn* offers detailed stock research, with free access to Zacks Investment Research and quarterly sector re-ports from Argus Research. You can get fundamental statistical data on thousands of companies, as well as cash flow statements, income statements, and balance sheets. The site also provides help-ful articles on investing and timely columns to help investors man-age their Folios.

- *Preselected Folios.* This is one of the site's greatest strengths. It offers well over 100 preselected Folios that you can use for your own portfolio. The Folios include large, mid-cap, and small stocks; foreign stocks; ethical stocks; and specialized sectors.

- *Folio wizard.* An interactive Folio wizard helps customers determine their investment profile, select the right asset mix, and pick the appropriate Folios for their accounts.

- *Customer care.* FOLIO*fn* offers assistance through a toll-free help line and online e-mail.

Other Highlights

- *No minimum balance required.* Investors can start with any amount.

- *Partial shares.* FOLIO*fn* allows investors to buy partial shares, slowly, steadily building a position in a portfolio of stocks through dollar cost averaging.

- *Tax tracking.* The company's tax tracking system shows you exactly where you stand on tax gains and losses with each holding in your account.

- *IRAs and custodial accounts are available.*

- *Automatic investment.* Many FOLIO*fn* customers use dollar cost averaging by adding to their accounts through automatic electronic withdrawals from their checking or savings accounts or through a payroll deduction plan.

- *Online account histories.* Statements and account opening and transaction histories are stored online.

- *Track and monitor your account online.*

BUYANDHOLD.COM

BUYandHOLD.com has been a true groundbreaker in the flat-rate brokerage business, although it does not offer preselected Folios. The New York–based operation was the first brokerage firm to offer dollar-based investing and fractional share purchases for stocks on all the major exchanges. BUYandHOLD was acquired by Fahnestock Viner

Holdings in January 2002, although it continues to operate as a separate entity. BUYandHOLD claims more than 125,000 customers.

The company offers three payment options. For $14.99 a month, you can make unlimited buy-and-sell window trades. For $6.99 a month, you get two free buy or sell window trades each month and must pay only $2.99 for any additional window trades. Real-time trades will cost you $19.99.

Since it opened in November 1999, BUYandHOLD has been one of the fastest growing brokerages in the online business. It is the nation's tenth largest online broker in terms of customer accounts and daily transactions. BUYandHOLD has drawn wide praise from the financial media. It was a "Best of the Web" pick by Forbes.com online magazine, *U.S. News & World Report,* and *Mutual Funds* magazine in 2000.

As its name implies, BUYandHOLD focuses on long-term-oriented investors, with an emphasis on dollar cost averaging. As *Online Investor* magazine put it: "BUYandHOLD has taken a first-to-the-market advantage and created a full menu of services for the dollar-based investor. Besides getting cheap trades for stock purchases as small as $20, you get assistance setting up custodial accounts for minors, investment club advice, and educational articles."

Although BUYandHOLD does not offer preselected Folios, it does give investors access to three inexpensive online investment advisory services that do recommend promising stocks for individual portfolios.

Fees

BUYandHOLD.com offers these options:

- *Monthly subscription fee.* For just $14.99 a month, you can make unlimited buy-and-sell window purchases in your account, and you can have money from your bank or other account automatically invested in stocks at no additional charge.

- *Lower monthly fee.* Infrequent traders may opt for the second option. For $6.99 a month, you get two free window trades and the opportunity to make any additional trades for just $2.99 per transaction.

- *Real-time transactions.* If you want to buy and sell stocks at the current market price, you pay a fee of $19.99 per transaction, which is similar to other online brokers.

- *Window trades.* Window trades are made three times a day. The company offers window trades on more than 4,000 stocks.

Investment Assistance

- *Some on-site stock research.* This is not a strong point. Although there are some research data on individual stocks available at BUYandHOLD.com, it is very sketchy. If you need to do serious research on a stock, you will need to go to Yahoo! (finance), Hoovers, AOL, or another investment site.

- *Investment articles.* BUYandHOLD offers a large archive of articles on investing, along with some weekly columns designed to help investors choose stocks wisely.

- *Subscription advisory services.* BUYandHOLD does not list any preselected portfolios, such as the ones at FOLIO*fn,* but it does offer customers the option of subscribing to three inexpensive on-line advisory services that do offer stock recommendations. One service, Stocks to Start, costs just $14.99 the first year, while the Portfolio Picks service costs $19.99 the first year, and In-Depth Insights costs $24.99 the first year. All three services are designed to give investors ideas on stocks to add to their portfolios.

- *Customer care.* BUYandHOLD offers online e-mail customer assistance and a toll-free phone number.

Other Highlights

- *No minimum balance required.* Investors can start with any amount.

- *Partial shares.* BUYandHOLD allows investors to buy partial shares, slowly, steadily building a position in a portfolio of stocks.

- *IRAs and custodial accounts are available.*

- *Automatic investment.* Many BUYandHOLD customers use dollar cost averaging by adding to their account through automatic electronic withdrawals from their checking or savings accounts, or through a payroll deduction plan. Through its dollar cost averaging program, investors can contribute a minimum of $20 per period (weekly, monthly, or quarterly) to any or all the stocks in the portfolio.

- *Online account histories.* Statements and account opening and transaction histories are stored online.

- *Track and monitor your account online.*

SHAREBUILDER.COM

ShareBuilder.com may be just fine for investors who want to buy stocks, but it's not so good for those who want to buy *and sell* their shares. The company was launched in 1999 and is a wholly owned subsidiary of NetStock Corporation.

The company offers a flat monthly fee of just $12 for all the stock purchases you want to make, but charges you $15.95 per transaction whenever you want to sell a stock. Long-term-oriented investors may not be concerned about the additional sell fee, but those who like to tinker with their portfolios would probably be better served trying a different service. The company does offer some preselected portfolio options for customers that mirror some of the major stock indexes.

One other serious drawback to ShareBuilder: Window trades are made only once a week (Tuesdays). If you order a stock on Wednesday, you'll have to wait a full week for your trade to go through. A lot could happen in the market in a week. By comparison, FOLIO*fn* and E*Trade make window trades twice a day, and BUYandHOLD.com makes trades three times a day.

Fees

ShareBuilder.com offers these options:

- *Monthly subscription fee.* For $12 per month, you can make unlimited window purchases in your account. However, you must pay $15.95 to sell a stock from the account.

- *Low single transaction fee.* If you wish, you can skip the monthly fee and just pay a low transaction fee of $4 for each window purchase—and $15.95 for each sale.

- *Real-time transactions.* If you want to buy and sell stocks at the current market price, you pay a fee of $15.95 per transaction, which is similar to other online brokers.

- *Window trades.* Window stock purchases are made just once a week (on Tuesdays), which compares poorly to ShareBuilder's leading rivals, who execute window trades two or three times a day. ShareBuilder offers window trades on more than 4,000 stocks.

Investment Assistance

- *Personal portfolio building guidelines.* The ShareBuilder site offers a portfolio planning tool called PlanBuilder that helps investors determine their investment profile and threshold for risk through a series of questions. Once the investor completes the survey, PlanBuilder offers a recommended asset allocation mix and guides you to its preselected investment baskets to help you construct your own portfolio.

- *Preselected baskets.* ShareBuilder offers several preselected portfolios that are based on the major stock indexes, including portfolios that mirror the Dow Jones Industrial Average, the Standard & Poor's 500, the Nasdaq 100, the S&P MidCap 400, the S&P SmallCap 600, and the Russell 3000.

- *Customer care.* ShareBuilder offers online e-mail customer assistance, which I found to be very prompt, and a phone number to call for help, which was not so prompt—after 30 minutes on hold, I gave up.

- *Some on-site stock research.* This is not a strong point. Although there is some research data on individual stocks available at ShareBuilder.com, it is very limited. If you need to do serious research on a stock, you will have to go elsewhere on the Web.

Other Highlights

- *Investors can buy fractional shares.*

- *No minimum balance required.* Investors can start with any amount

- *Partial shares.* ShareBuilder allows investors to buy partial shares, slowly, steadily building a position in a portfolio of stocks.

- *IRAs and custodial accounts are available.*

- *Automatic investment.* Many ShareBuilder customers add to their accounts through automatic electronic withdrawals from their checking or savings accounts or through a payroll deduction plan. Customers can use the dollar cost averaging option to add regularly to their positions through automatic electronic withdrawals.

- *Online account histories.* Statements and account opening and transaction histories are stored online.

- *Track and monitor your account online.*

E*TRADE

E*Trade has joined the stock basket revolution, although its service falls short of its rivals in some key areas.

E*Trade's fee structure is dramatically different from other stock basket brokers. The company charges an annual fee based on a percentage of assets in the account rather than as a flat monthly or yearly fee. And unlike its online competitors, the E*Trade Stock Basket program requires not only a $5,000 minimum investment to open the account (except in IRA accounts), it also requires a $500 subsequent investment minimum. That means that the dollar cost averaging approach won't work for many small investors who would have a hard time coughing up $500 a month for each of the stocks in their portfolio.

E*Trade uses a graduated rate structure for its Stock Basket service, which is based on the size of the customer's account. It charges 1.25 percent per year for accounts of under $50,000, 1 percent per year on accounts of $50,000 to $100,000, and 0.75 percent on accounts of $100,000 or above. Here's how it breaks down in dollar terms:

Account Size	Annual Fee
$ 10,000	$ 125 (1.25%)
20,000	250 (1.25%)
40,000	500 (1.25%)
75,000	750 (1%)
100,000	750 (0.75%)
500,000	3,750 (0.75%)
1,000,000	7,500 (0.75%)

As you can see, the E*Trade Stock Basket service would cost more than other online services for all but the smallest investors.

E*Trade makes window trades twice daily. It offers several off-the-shelf portfolios, including index-type Folios that represent the Dow 30, the Nasdaq 25, the S&P 20, the S&P 25 MidCap, and the S&P 30 SmallCap. It also has about ten sector baskets and several other large, mid-cap, and small stock baskets.

E*Trade does offer better stock research capabilities than most of its online rivals, but its Stock Basket program just doesn't stack up with the market leaders.

Fees

E*Trade offers these options:

- *Yearly fee based on percent of assets.* It charges 1.25 percent per year for accounts of under $50,000 (with a $50 per year minimum on small accounts), 1 percent per year on accounts of $50,000 to $100,000, and 0.75 percent on accounts of $100,000 or above.

E*Trade gives you unlimited buy-and-sell window purchases in your account, and you can have money from your bank or other account automatically invested in your basket stocks for free.

- *Real-time transactions.* If you want to buy and sell stocks at the current market price, you pay a fee of $19.95 per transaction for Nasdaq stocks and $14.95 for stocks traded on major exchanges.

- *Window trades are made twice a day.* The company offers window trades on more than 4,000 stocks.

Investment Assistance

- *In-depth stock research.* E*Trade offers in-depth research on thousands of stocks, including stock growth charts, fundamentals, earnings and revenue history, earnings projections, SEC filings, and other information. It also offers stock screening tools and special features and stock picks from the experts.

- *Investor education.* E*Trade offers the "Knowledge Center" with an archive of helpful articles on how to invest in stocks. It also publishes timely articles on the market and on individual stocks and sectors.

- *Preselected baskets.* E*Trade offers several off-the-shelf portfolios, including index-type Folios that represent the Dow 30, the Nasdaq 25, the S&P 20, the S&P 25 MidCap, and the S&P 30 SmallCap. It also has about ten sector baskets and several other large, mid-cap, and small stock baskets.

- *Customer care.* E*Trade offers online e-mail customer assistance and a toll-free phone number.

Other Highlights

- The basket program requires a minimum investment of $5,000, except IRA accounts, which require a $2,000 investment minimum.

- *Buy stocks in dollars.* You can purchase partial shares of a stock, buying stocks in dollars rather than shares.

- *IRAs and custodial accounts are available.*

- *Track and monitor your account online.*

FIDELITY

Fidelity Investments, a powerhouse in both the mutual fund and on-line discount brokerage businesses, has made a tepid effort to throw its hat into the stock basket ring.

Although the company pushes the concept of creating your own basket of up to 50 stocks, it offers no free or discounted trades. You pay the full $25 commission on all trades, including stock purchases to build your basket and all additional purchases to add to your positions. That defeats the purpose of the Folio concept.

Investors also are required to have an account minimum of $10,000 before opening a basket.

Fidelity offers no preselected baskets. Instead, investors are invited to build their own baskets. To its credit, the Fidelity site offers an excellent database of stock research and screening tools. But the Fidelity Stock Basket program on its own offers customers little reason to enroll.

Fees

Fidelity offers its Stock Basket customers the same commission rate schedule as it does its online customers:

- *Standard rate.* $25 per trade for the first 1,000 shares and 2 cents per share for each additional share.

- *Silver level.* $14.95 per trade (for the first 1,000 shares and 1.5 cents per share for each additional share) for customers with at least $100,000 in the account or for those who make at least 36 trades per year.

- *Gold level.* $14 per trade (for the first 1,000 shares and 1 cent per share for each additional share) for those with at least $2 million in the account or who make at least 240 trades per year.

Investment Assistance

- *In-depth stock research.* Fidelity offers research on thousands of stocks, including stock growth charts, financial histories, analyst ratings, fundamentals, and other information. It also offers stock screening tools.

- *Investor education.* Fidelity offers timely articles on the market and on individual stocks and sectors.

- *No preselected baskets.* Fidelity does not offer off-the-shelf baskets for customers, but it does allow customers to set up their own "watch baskets," so that they can follow potential investments before actually investing any money.

Other Highlights

- *The basket program requires an account minimum of $10,000, but there is no minimum subsequent investment requirement.*

- *Track and monitor your account online.*

FREETRADE.COM

Freetrade.com is not a Folio or stock basket brokerage, but it does offer free online trades—both to buy and sell. So you could use Freetrade .com as a site to buy baskets of stocks and add to your holdings through dollar cost averaging (although you cannot buy partial shares through Freetrade.com).

Even though the trades are free, the site definitely has its drawbacks. Forget about on-site investment research information. And Freetrade has no phone line, so you can't talk with a friendly customer representative.

The company has other restrictions, as well. It accepts wire transfers only—no checks or money orders—because the company has no one in the office to open mail from customers. All business is conducted by e-mail. Nor does Freetrade offer IRAs or other retirement accounts, mutual funds, bonds, or over-the-counter stocks. However, some investors who have used the site say the trade execution measures up with other online brokers.

Freetrade, which is owned by Ameritrade Holdings, has kept its services to a minimum in order to offer trades for free. As the company reports at its Web site: "Every cost not necessary for executing stock trades has been eliminated." The company spends almost nothing on marketing and advertising, relying instead on word of mouth. It spends even less on customer service personnel. According to its Web site: "We do not have a telephone or office location for customer service. We also do not have people assigned to open mail."

The firm does charge $5 for stop and limit orders and odd lots. It also generates some revenue through other means, including interest on margin accounts, advertising on its the Web site, and order flow payments from market makers and specialists. The company requires a $5,000 minimum to open an account.

Fees

Freetrade.com has two options:

1. *Free for market trades.*

2. *$5 for stop and limit orders and odd lots.*

Investment Assistance

- *No stock research.* The company offers no investment research information at its Web site.

- *No preselected baskets of stocks.*

- *Very limited customer care.* You cannot call a service representative, because the company has no phone line. But the firm does respond to e-mail questions.

- *No bonds, mutual funds, or over-the-counter stocks sold at the site.*

- *No checks or money orders accepted.* Freetrade accepts wire transfers only; no stock certificates are delivered and no transfers allowed.

- *No IRAs or other retirement accounts are available.*

- *Not available to Macintosh users—Windows users only.*

- *A $5,000 minimum account balance is required.*

- *Track and monitor your account online.*

BROKERAGEAMERICA.COM

Like Freetrade.com, BrokerageAmerica.com offers free stock trades for online investors but very little else in the way of service. However, unlike Freetrade, BrokerageAmerica does allow you to send checks and money orders, it does have a customer phone line, and you can get broker-assisted trades (for $14.95 per trade). The company also offers IRA accounts, mutual funds, and bonds.

The company does not offer preselected stock baskets.

BrokerageAmerica customers have given the Web site mixed reviews. The biggest complaint has been difficulty opening an account. The firm's trade execution process has drawn some positive and negative comments from users who reported their experiences at an online brokerage review site. (See <www.sonic.net/donaldj> for more details.)

How does BrokerageAmerica make money? The company explains it this way: "We can do this because we're set up as a market maker, providing liquidity through large-scale market making operations. So when you trade with us, you're dealing directly with a market maker. As a market maker, we make money by providing liquidity, assuming risk, and from a portion of the difference between the bid and offer price for a stock, the way market makers always have."

The company also generates revenue by charging one of the highest margin interest rates in the online brokerage business. BrokerageAmerica requires an account minimum of $1,000.

Fees

BrokerageAmerica.com has several options:

- *Free market trades.*

- *$5 for stop and limit orders.*

- *$14.95 for broker-assisted market trades and $19.95 for broker-assisted stop and limit orders.*

Investment Assistance

- *No stock research available.* The Web site does not offer research on stocks and funds but refers interested investors to other sites that specialize in research.

- *No preselected baskets of stocks.*

- *Does not sell fractional shares.* Must buy stock in shares, not dollars.

- *Customer care.* BrokerageAmerica offers assistance through e-mail and a toll-free phone number.

- *In addition to stocks and options, the company sells bonds, mutual funds, small over-the-counter stocks, and some foreign stocks.*

- *A $1,000 minimum account balance is required.*

- *Track and monitor your account online.*

The Folio market has been changing rapidly, so pricing and services at some of these companies may have changed by the time you read this. The best test is to do some Web surfing of your own. Check out each of the sites and decide which company works best for you.

CHAPTER 3

BUILDING YOUR OWN
PERSONAL FOLIO

F inally, you have the financial freedom to play in the same league as the big market makers on Wall Street. You can build your own diversified portfolio of outstanding stocks— or several different portfolios. You decide what to buy, when to buy it, and, if necessary, when to sell it. But that privilege can be both a pleasure and a pain.

With opportunity comes responsibility. Building your own diversified portfolio requires extensive research on dozens or hundreds of stocks. That takes time, effort, and a well-designed strategy. And the work doesn't end there. Once you've constructed your portfolio, you must continue to monitor all of your stocks to decide which to hold, which to sell, and which other stocks to add to your portfolio.

Labor-intensive as it may sound, however, investing is a passion for millions of individuals who truly enjoy following their stocks and monitoring the market. In a sense, your portfolio is your own little dynasty, your own small piece of America's greatest companies, your own thin slice of the American pie.

This chapter will guide you through the portfolio-building process. We'll review some of the most important principles of investing and focus on which types of stocks and industrial sectors may be most appropriate for your investment dollars. We'll also examine some fundamental precepts in buying, selling, and analyzing individual stocks. Nothing in this chapter will make you millions overnight, but you will develop a realistic approach to investing based on time-tested fundamentals that will yield the best success in the stock market over the long term.

RULES 1, 2, AND 3: DIVERSIFY, DIVERSIFY, DIVERSIFY

As Yogi Berra once said: "When you come to a fork in the road, take it." That same sage advice applies to stock market investing. Branch out in every direction possible. Buy the best stocks in all the best industries. No matter how broadly you diversify, in truth, you'll still take some hits along the way. That's how the stock market works. But a broadly diversified portfolio can keep the tremors to a minimum.

There is no bigger benefit to the new Folio concept than the ability to diversify. Whereas most small investors in the past had to settle for a portfolio of 5 to 15 stocks, Folios allow investors to buy dozens of stocks for the same low annual fee.

Study after study of investment strategies has concluded that the biggest key to long-term success in the stock market is diversification. Diversification may mean different things to different investment managers, but generally speaking, a truly diversified portfolio will include stocks from 10 to 20 industrial sectors and subsectors. It might include foods, retailers, medical, computers, telecommunications, consumer goods, transportation, energy, manufacturing, and financial services. In some cases, you may want to own several different stocks from the same sector, which means that, in all, your portfolio may include 30 to 50 stocks.

But there is no reason to rush the buying process. You don't need to start with a full portfolio. Take your time. Start with the companies you know well, even if that's only a handful of stocks. Then gradually add to your holdings as your research leads you to other stocks that meet your criteria.

Although it's important to diversify across several industry groups, it only makes sense to put a greater share of your investment dollars in the faster growing industries. While technology stocks have been battered relentlessly in recent years, the tech sector has dramatically outperformed the overall market over the past 10 to 20 years. In the years ahead, technology probably will continue to be the fastest growing area of the economy because of innovations and advances that technology industries will bring.

Some ambitious investors also may want to build a specialized portfolio, such as a tech stock Folio or a Folio of high dividend stocks. Portfolios that focus on a small slice of the economy can provide outstanding returns when that particular sector is in favor, but specialized portfolios tend to be very volatile.

LEADING SECTORS

When deciding which sectors to invest in, try to focus on long-term economic trends rather than short-term strengths and weaknesses. Let's evaluate some of the leading sectors based on their long-term prospects.

Oil, Gas, and Related Energy Stocks

The energy sector always becomes a very popular play when oil prices start to climb. And why not? Owning oil stocks can help put a smile on your face every time prices go up at the pump. Unfortunately, oil and natural gas stocks tend to be very cyclical, climbing quickly when oil prices move up and tailing off when prices dip back down. In fact, many investors who play the oil and gas sector tend to buy into the sector too late to cash in on the higher prices. Energy stocks tend to go up rapidly just as oil prices start moving up, but investors who are late to the party often end up buying those stocks at the peak, only to watch share prices edge back down when oil prices level off or decline.

If you do invest in energy stocks, do it because of their long-term potential, not because of a short-term energy crunch. There is certainly some justification for owning oil or gas stocks as part of a diversified portfolio. Although energy stocks have not been among the market leaders over the past two decades, they have had some big spurts along the way. And the future of the oil and gas industry seems solid. There's only a finite amount of this vital commodity in the world, and when supplies start to dwindle, the prices could skyrocket. How soon will that happen? Theories abound, but none is conclusive. Now that Russia has begun tapping its enormous oil reserves, the world's oil supply seems stable for the moment. But that could change over the next decade or two. And as history has shown us, certain world events can dramatically affect short-term oil prices. That's when it's nice to have a stake in oil or gas stocks. You can choose from among the big, well-known conglomerates, such as ExxonMobil and ChevronTexaco, or the smaller oil drilling companies, such as Global Marine. You also can play the energy market by investing in alternative energy stocks, such as solar cell developer AstroPower. Most of the stocks of the energy sector tend to trade in tandem, moving up when oil prices are on the rise and leveling off or falling when oil prices decline.

How much should you invest in energy companies? Because energy stocks have not been among the market leaders historically, there's no need to overcommit yourself. You may wish to keep your energy investment modest—perhaps 5 to 10 percent of the portfolio.

Medical and Biotechnology

Medical companies have been among the leading stocks in the market for many decades and should continue to flourish for years to come. Health care is virtually recession-proof. Consumers will spend their last dollar—and even take on debt—to keep themselves healthy.

There are several key subsectors in the medical area:

- The traditional pharmaceutical companies, such as Merck, Pfizer, and Bristol-Myers Squibb

- Medical technology companies, such as Medtronic, which makes heart pacemakers and other implantable medical devices

- Biotechnology companies that focus on genetic medications, such as Amgen, Genentech, and Affymetrix

- Hospital, medical center, and nursing home chains, such as Universal Health

- HMOs and other physician organizations, such as United Health

Although there are profitable companies in each medical subsector, the pharmaceutical and medical technology companies have traditionally been the most successful. Many of the leading firms have managed to post annual earnings growth of 15 to 25 percent consistently for many years. As a result, pharmaceutical and medical technology stocks have long been a favorite of investors and money managers.

It's the biotechnology companies that may have the biggest future. The mapping of the genetic code has opened up a new world of medical technology. Experts in the medical field are exploring new cancer cures, cloned organ transplants, the prevention of birth defects, and a wide range of other medical advances that biotechnology could bring.

Several stocks in the biotech sector, such as Genentech and Amgen, are already making money, and many of those that aren't have been posting exceptional revenue growth. One of the most promising areas of biotech research is the quest for new and better cancer treatments. There are more than 120 forms of cancer, and traditional treatments such as chemotherapy have never been particularly successful. Not only is the cure rate for most forms of treatment unacceptably low, but the treatments also lead to a number of disturbing side effects, such as nausea, hair loss, removal of body parts, and the weakening of the body and its functions. But new advances in biotechnology could lead to cancer cures with a much higher success rate—without the side effects. Further development of cancer cures and other biotech therapies should lead to huge profits for the companies that get their products to market ahead of the pack.

The other medical subsectors, medical care providers and HMOs, have had some success, although not at the same level as the pharmaceutical and medical technology companies. But they still should be considered in your portfolio selection process. In all, health care stocks should account for at least 10 percent of your portfolio—and as much as 30 percent for more aggressive investors.

Automotive and Transportation

Why punish yourself? The automotive and transportation industry has underperformed the overall market for several decades. Ford and

General Motors may enjoy an occasional run-up, but over the long term those stocks have been very disappointing. Harley-Davidson has been the only good stock in the automotive sector over the past ten years (although some analysts consider Harley a recreational stock rather than automotive).

Related industries have not fared much better. Even before the 9-11 attacks, the airline sector had been through years of market turbulence. Southwest Airlines has been the only major carrier to post increasing earnings and revenue on a consistent basis. Boeing, the world's leading airplane manufacturer, also has experienced a volatile history, climbing with every big order and declining with every downturn in the airline industry. Five percent of your portfolio is probably plenty for this sector.

Food and Beverages

We all get hungry, and there's an entire industry feasting every day on your appetite. The food and beverage industry makes up a vast and never-ending share of our economy. There are several important subsectors within the food industry, including:

- *Food and beverage production.* Many of the top American food and beverage companies have been around for many decades and sell their products worldwide. Among the leaders are Coca-Cola, PepsiCo, Sara Lee, Hershey's, and ConAgra.

- *Restaurants and food services.* McDonald's has been the most successful of all restaurant chains around the world, but others also have had solid runs. Generally, stocks of the older restaurant chains tend to become fairly sluggish as they reach the saturation point around the country with their restaurants. It is best to invest in restaurants in their early stages and sell out when the growth starts to slow.

- *Grocery stores.* A number of grocery store chains have enriched investors over the years, including Safeway, Kroger, and Albertson's.

- *Alcoholic beverages.* There is only one significant blue chip stock in the alcoholic beverage market, Anheuser-Busch. The other leading brewer, Miller Beer, is owned by Philip Morris and accounts for a relatively small part of the company's overall financial returns. Anheuser-Busch has been one of the most consistent companies in America over the past 30 years.

Consumer Staples

Not only do we have to eat and drink, we also need to brush our teeth, bathe, wash our clothes, and clean our homes. That's not going to change, which is why the consumer staples sector should draw some of your investment dollars. Consumer staples companies such as Procter & Gamble, Gillette, and Newell-Rubbermaid have had mixed results in recent years, but their long-term records have been very solid. All are dominant players in the global consumer market, with sales in dozens of countries. Don't expect huge stock gains in this sector, but you certainly have reason to anticipate solid returns for years to come. A diversified portfolio should have at least 5 percent of assets in consumer staples.

Retail

The retail sector has always been a vital part of the American economy. Retail stocks tend to do best in the months closest to Christmas, for obvious reasons. Investors begin to think about retail stocks as the holidays approach and then continue that interest through the first quarter of the following year, when retailers release their holiday sales and earnings figures. Very little happens in retail over the spring and summer quarters.

Retail operations usually enjoy their largest growth in their early years before they have saturated the market with outlets. However, a top line retailer can enjoy many years of expansion before reaching the saturation point. Wal-Mart averaged 40 percent annual earnings growth for its first 30 years as a publicly traded company. Home Depot, Best Buy, Kohl's, Starbucks, and Walgreen have also enjoyed many years of rising earnings and revenue.

Many other retailers have seen their growth rate slow dramatically once their expansion ebbed. Montgomery Ward went out of business, while JC Penney, Kmart, and Sears have encountered some rough waters, along with many other national retailers. So if you buy retail stock, buy a company that is either early in its expansion process or a market leader, such as Home Depot or Wal-Mart, which have continued to post consistent growth year in and year out. Retail stocks might make up 5 to 15 percent of a well-diversified portfolio.

Financial

Boring as they may seem, insurance companies, investment companies, banks, and other financial services companies have been very steady performers over the long term. Here are the key subsectors of the financial industry:

- *Banks and lending organizations.* After a slump in the 1980s, the banking industry has been one of the strongest, most profitable sectors of the American economy since the early 1990s. Large national and regional banks as well as smaller banking organizations have continued to rack up impressive earnings growth for the past few years. Two other related operations, Fannie Mae and Freddie Mac, are among the leaders in the mortgage lending market and have posted many years of record earnings.

- *Insurance companies.* Some insurance companies took a big hit with the 9-11 terrorist attacks, but generally speaking, insurance companies have been pretty solid performers for many years.

- *Brokers and financial services companies.* The brokerage and financial services sector has been through many ups and downs. When the stock market is hot, these companies become very profitable, but market slumps can create serious financial pain for brokers. Among the leaders in this industry are Merrill Lynch, T. Rowe Price, Franklin Resources, and Alliance Capital Management.

- *Credit card companies.* Some financial organizations specialize in issuing credit cards, such as MBNA, which is the nation's leading credit card lender. Those companies have done well in the market in recent years and could do even better if new, more restrictive rules on credit card bankruptcy are enacted.

Conservative investors should have at least 10 percent of assets in financial stocks.

Chemicals and Coatings

This has been one of the more stable sectors of the stock market for many years. Such market leaders as Sherwin-Williams and Valspar have racked up solid earnings growth year after year. Conservative investors may wish to put 5 to 10 percent of their assets in this sector.

Corporate Services

This is a broad-ranging category that includes some very successful companies across several subsectors. Some of the leading areas of the corporate services sectors include:

- *Payroll services.* Automatic Data Processing (ADP) and Paychex are two of the world's leading payroll check processing companies and have posted impressive records of growth. In fact, ADP has posted more than 50 consecutive years of record sales and earnings— longer than any other company in America.

- *Data processing.* A number of companies provide a wide range of data processing services for other companies, including Fiserv, a data processing provider for banks and other financial institutions.

- *Advertising.* Omnicom Group and Interpublic Group are two of the world's leading advertising agencies and have posted very impressive returns over the past ten years.

- *Other.* A number of other solid companies also fit the corporate services category, including Cintas, which leases and sells workplace uniforms; Concorde EFS, which provides merchant card transaction processing; and ABM Industries, which provides such services as engineering, commercial security, parking facility management, and mechanical services.

The corporate services sector should be appropriate for about 5 to 15 percent of your portfolio.

Telecommunications

At last we get to the telecommunications sector. Once one of the hottest sectors of the economy, telecom has caused great pain for investors in recent years. A severe slump in the telecommunications industry caused a dip in earnings and revenue growth for most of the manufacturers in the telecom market. The downturn sent several market leaders, such as Lucent Technologies and ADC Telecommunications, to the brink of bankruptcy. Does that make it a sector to avoid? Not for those with a long-term perspective.

Once the industry recovers, telecom should once again become one of the fastest growing industries in the global economy. Nations around the world will need to continue to upgrade their telecommunications infrastructure to provide phone service for new customers and other advanced telecommunications services for their existing customers.

The telecom industry includes both the manufacturers of phones and communications equipment and carriers, such as AT&T, MCI, and Qwest, that provide long-distance or local service to customers. The carriers generally have provided steady but unspectacular returns for shareholders for many years, while manufacturers experienced years of outstanding growth before falling victim to the technology market meltdown.

Conservative investors would be more likely to lean toward carriers, while aggressive investors may want to roll the dice on the telecom manufacturers. About 5 to 15 percent of a diversified portfolio should be telecom stocks.

Computer Technology

Like telecommunications, this sector has taken some severe lumps in recent years. A few software companies have avoided the huge plunge that most of the sector has endured, but most computer makers and semi-conductor, networking, and storage device manufacturers were badly whip-sawed in the market. Once the tech slump ends, however, many of these stocks could return to their former glory. Computer technology has been the fastest-growing sector of the economy for the past two decades and should continue to do well over the next two decades. Some of the leading computer technology subsectors include:

- *Computers.* The engine of the technology revolution, the computer may finally have reached a temporary saturation point with American consumers. But newer, more power-hungry software and Internet applications should prompt consumers to keep buying up-graded PCs. Advances in graphics also should keep sales moving for the new generation of monitors and color printers. Corporations and organizations also will need to update and replace old computer equipment and peripherals to keep up with the increasingly sophisticated enterprise software and e-commerce applications. Dell and IBM are leaders in computer sales for both consumers and businesses. Advances in graphics, voice and video applications, and expanded use of e-mail and e-commerce have also created a rapidly growing demand for data storage systems. Companies that make data storage devices, such as EMC and Advanced Digital Information Corp. (ADIC), have seen sales soar as organizations scramble to keep up with the increasing demand for data storage.

- *Semiconductors.* Also referred to as chips, microchips, or integrated circuits, semiconductors are the brains of the technology revolution. They are used to control a broad range of electronic devices, including computers, home appliances, machinery, automobiles, phones, remote control devices, and a growing legion of other products. Most chips are composed of a fingernail-sized sliver of silicon with layers of precise circuitry. The microchip market has been growing rapidly in recent years, although it has proven to be fairly cyclical.

- *Software.* Software serves as the operating system for computers and other types of electronic equipment and devices. Microsoft is the leader in the software market with its Windows operating software and its word processing, spreadsheet, financial, and other software applications. Oracle is the leader in business software, with a line of software for database and development, sales and service, manufacturing and supply chain, and finance and human resources applications. Other software companies offer software for a wide range of applications, including financial services and accounting, engineering and design, manufacturing and robotics, graphics, entertainment, and Web applications.

- *Networking.* Computer networking has become big business as large corporations and organizations add more applications and personnel to their already complex enterprise systems. Leaders in the networking sector, such as Foundry Networks and Brocade Communications, make products that tie together wide area networks (WANs) and local area networks (LANs).

- *The Internet.* Don't laugh. While most of the dot-coms have been pummeled into oblivion, the Internet will be with us for decades to come. Internet infrastructure companies such as Cisco, Juniper Networks, and Checkpoint Software should continue to grow. There is still a long, bright future for Internet-related companies.

Conservative investors should invest at least 10 to 15 percent of their assets in the rapidly expanding technology sector—spread across all the key subsectors—while aggressive investors may wish to go much higher.

Real Estate

Every time the stock market starts to slide, financial planners start pushing real estate–related investments such as REITs (real estate investment trusts) as a diversification tool. Think twice before you pour a lot of your money into this sector. Housing and commercial real estate prices were climbing quickly during the bull market, but much of that move was driven by the increase in wealth from rising stock prices. Now that many stocks have crashed and the dot-com millionaires have fallen back to earth, there's a lot less money available to fuel the real estate boom.

In Japan in the 1980s, real estate prices sky-rocketed along with stocks, but shortly after the stock market crashed, real estate valuations experienced their own meltdown. Imagine an investor who, after losing much of his or her money on stocks, switched his or her assets to real estate just in time for that market to tank. Could it happen here? Possibly. Besides, if you own a home, you've already got a pretty sizable investment in real estate. If you do decide to invest in REITs, keep it to no more than about 5 to 10 percent of your portfolio.

PICKING WINNERS IN THE MARKET

Investors use a lot of very different systems for picking stocks. And that, as they say, is what makes the market.

The approach I've always believed made the most sense was the same philosophy Winston Churchill used in all phases of his life. As Churchill once put it: "I'm easily satisfied with the very best." That should be your goal in the stock market. Be satisfied only with the very best—the all-star stocks of the fastest growing sectors. There are more than 10,000 stocks on the U.S. market. Even if you take your pick from the top 1 percent of the market, that still gives you more than 100 stocks from which to choose. There's no reason to settle for any stock that's average or below average.

But while that philosophy may sound obvious—buy the best and forget the rest—many investors never quite catch on. Some pick stocks based almost entirely on tips and personal sentiment. Others look for hidden values—stocks that may be trading at a low price relative to the rest of the market. Still others buy on momentum, grabbing shares of high-flying stocks as they start to surge. Those investment approaches can all work in the right market, but they have one common flaw: they overlook the single most important issue in picking a stock—is this a great pick for the long term?

Rather than selecting stocks based on short-term criteria, most investors should make their selections based on the quality of the company, its history, and its future prospects.

Look for companies that have become leaders in a fast-growing sector. Favor stocks with steadily growing revenue and earnings. There's no guarantee that strong stocks will stay strong, but what better companies on which to "bet" your money than profitable, growing companies that are dominant in their sectors? In reviewing the performance of the stocks in my book *The 100 Best Stocks to Own in America,* over seven editions dating back to 1989, those stocks, on average, outperformed the overall market averages edition after edition. There are no guarantees in the market, but blue chip companies with a strong history of financial growth will give the best chance of long-term success.

HOW TO RESEARCH STOCKS

It's simple to say "just buy the best," but how do you identify the best stocks in the market?

The first step is to find good prospects to investigate. There are plenty of sources available that provide leads for promising stocks, including *The 100 Best Stocks to Own in America,* the *Wall Street Journal, Money, Barron's, Investor's Business Daily, Kiplinger's Personal Finance, Worth, Forbes, Fortune,* and a long list of other financial publications. A number of financial Web sites also offer lists or screening tools that allow you to identify top stocks based on criteria you set. You also could use the special portfolios listed later in this book to cull your own prospect list.

Once you've identified a number of stocks for your prospect list, the next step is to do a thorough investigation of each stock. One of the best places to conduct your research is on the Internet.

There are many sites on the Web that provide extensive research on thousands of stocks. Yahoo!, AOL, MorningStar, OnMoney, and Hoovers are among the best, but there are many other outstanding sites as well. If you have an online brokerage account, you probably have access to extensive research, or if you open an account at an online Folio firm such as FOLIO*fn* or BUYandHOLD.com, you'll also have access to a wealth of investment information.

Here are some specific factors to look for when researching stocks on the Internet:

- *Financial history and fundamentals.* Look through the company's financial information. Are its revenues rising quickly and steadily? Does it have earnings? If so, are its earnings per share rising consistently? Look for companies that have racked up five to ten years of rising earnings and revenue. Make sure that the most recent quarters are still showing solid growth. Check the price-earnings ratio (PE) and see how it compares with other stocks in the same sector. PEs vary dramatically, which is why it's best to compare them to other stocks of the same sector. (See more on PEs on page 55.) The faster the company's earnings are growing, the higher the PE it can support. The same is true for the price-sales ratio. The faster the sales growth, the higher the price-sales ratio it can support. Very fast-growing companies may have a price-sales ratio of 50 to 100, but most companies are in the range of 1 to 5. Retailers and distributors, which have high sales and low margins, generally have price-sales ratios of less than 1. If the company's financial history and basic fundamentals look good, following are some other online information you should examine.

- *Chart.* Click on the company's stock growth history chart to see how the stock has been doing for the past three to five years. If it has been relatively flat for several years, that's a bad sign. If it has had a general upward trend—even with some volatility—that's a good sign.

- *News.* Click on "News" to find out more about the company. Often, you will see the headlines for several news stories. Look for articles on recent quarterly earnings reports. There you can find out how the company has been doing financially, and what areas have been its strengths. Usually, those articles also quote the CEO, who gives his or her assessment of the company's performance. The CEO always tries to put a positive spin on the performance, but if it sounds like he or she is apologizing or making excuses, that's a bad sign. Often at the bottom of those articles, you can find a long paragraph describing the company and its products or services, which you may find helpful. Also look for other news articles that can give you information on new products, new customers, or new corporate alliances. If the company is doing business with other prominent companies, that's a good sign.

- *Web site.* Check out the company's Web site. If you don't know the site name, open your search engine and type in the name of the company. The browser will lead you to the site. Once at the site, there are many things you can look for. You can usually find a good corporate profile, press releases dating back several months or years, a list of products or services, and other relevant information about the company. You can also link into the company's Securities and Exchange Commission filings. Look for the most recent annual or 10-K report. Those reports often cover 50 to 100 pages, with very specific details of the company's business, its products or services, and even its leading customers and competitors. It also provides information on the officers of the company, the company's research and development efforts, its sales and distribution system, expansion plans, manufacturing operations, and other pertinent data.

You also may wish to page through the company's annual report. What do you look for? There are some fairly simple keys you can look for, as the following section explains.

Analyzing Corporate Annual Reports

In addition to the wealth of information you can learn about a company on the Internet, you also may want to examine a company's annual report. But it's important to focus on substance, not sizzle. Dazzling artwork, flowery praise, and bold predictions are sometimes used to camouflage ho-hum financial returns.

There are investors who like to study every detail of a report's financial section, combing through the balance sheet, the cash flow figures, and the footnotes in search of any undiscovered nuggets that could help them decide whether the company is destined for stellar performance. In truth, that effort isn't going to yield anything that the analysts on Wall Street didn't already know months before. Just the same, there are important points you can consider in making your own decision about a company.

Generally speaking, you can get an excellent idea of a company's recent success within the first two or three pages of the report—based on what they show or, just as important, what they don't show. The deeper you have to page into a report to find anything on the company's financial results, the worse those results are likely to be. But if the returns have been stellar, you can rest assured the company will put it right up front.

In most cases, companies publish three graphs near the front of the book—one showing *revenue* (or sales) growth over the past few years, one showing *net income* growth, and one showing *earnings per share* growth. In reviewing those graphs, you can find out if the company has enjoyed steady, consistent growth in recent years. If those three graphs are not featured in the first few pages, be suspicious. It often means the company has something to hide—like substandard growth rates. Often, companies will put in other graphs, such as growth of number of employees, assets, inventory, or cash and cash investments—anything the corporate PR people can think of to show some type of positive growth. But beware: If the report doesn't show revenue, net income, and earnings per share, any other graphs are likely just a cover-up.

Sometimes, the report will open with brilliant graphics designed to convey success. Again, it's just fool's gold—sort of like a Hollywood movie: the more dazzling the special effects, the weaker the plot.

What else is worth reading in an annual report? Here are some other areas to examine:

- *Balance sheet.* You should probably spend a few minutes skimming through the balance sheet to see whether the company is showing steady growth in key areas such as *assets, sales, earnings,* and *book value.*

- *Financial history.* Many company reports also give a five- to ten-year history of such financial data as *revenue, assets, dividends, net income,* and *earnings per share.* Also, look at gross profit, long-term debt, and operating income to make sure the company's financial strength remains solid. The financial history data sheet is a great place to determine whether the company has had a long history of consistent financial growth—or one that bounces around from year to year. Obviously, the most attractive companies are those that show solid growth of key financials year in and year out.

- *Company information.* Annual reports also can give you an idea of what the company does and how successful it is at doing it. They often describe the company's products or services, its customers, and its expansion strategies. Although most of the information is little more than hype written by the company's PR department, it still can give you a sense of the company's business.

- *Letter to shareholders.* Annual reports always include a letter to shareholders from the company president, CEO, or chairman. Be warned, however, that those letters typically give the most positive possible spin on the company's operations. Read them with a skeptical eye.

If you're interested in even more details of a company's operations, you may find the 10-K report to be more helpful than the annual report. Unlike annual reports, 10-K reports have no fluff and no photos—just facts. Printed on plain white paper, with page after page of single-spaced copy, the 10-K provides a factual profile of the company, with details on its history, its industry, its corporate marketing strategy, its product mix, its distribution system, its customers, its competitors, its employees, its key officers, and its international operations. Any significant lawsuits the company is involved in also will be mentioned in the 10-K. For some reason, however, the 10-K report companies send to interested investors is often a condensed version of the 10-K report filed with the SEC that is posted on the Internet.

How do you get a company's annual and 10-K reports? It's usually as simple as asking for them. Call or write the company and request its most recent annual report, 10-K report, and quarterly reports. The company usually will send them to you at no charge (although in recent years some companies have asked that you go to their Web site to find copies of their reports because of the added expense of printing and mailing the reports).

WALL STREET'S FAVORITE QUOTIENT

Cheap stocks are all a matter of perspective. On Wall Street, a low stock price doesn't necessarily mean the stock is cheap. In fact, in value terms, a $100 stock could be cheaper than a $3 stock. It all depends on the *price-earnings ratio.*

The price-earnings ratio—known in the business as the PE—is the most commonly used measure of a stock's value. Many professionals and individual investors decide which stocks to buy and sell based largely on the PE. (The PEs are listed every day in the stock tables of most major newspapers, as well as at nearly any Internet financial site.) Investors often watch the PEs as closely as the stock price itself. It's a measure every serious investor should understand.

Literally translated, the price-earnings ratio means *the stock price divided by the earnings per share.* For example, a $10 stock with annual earnings of $1 per share would have a PE of 10 ($10 divided by $1).

Which of the following stocks would be cheaper in Wall Street terms?

- A $20 stock with earnings of $1 per share (a PE of 20)?

- A $100 stock with earnings of $10 a share (a PE of 10)?

In value terms, the $100 stock would be cheaper than the $20 stock, because the PE of the $100 stock is half that of the $20 stock.

PEs are a lot like golf scores—the lower the better. Most established blue chip stocks have PEs in the range of 10 to 30. The average PE for a stock on the Dow Jones Industrial Average over the past 50 years has been about 13, although over the past 10 years that figure has climbed to about 18. In fact, the average PE jumped to over 20 during the bull market run of the late 1990s. Analysts believe that was one of the reasons the market dropped so severely in 2000 and 2001.

In comparing PEs, think of buying a stock in much the same way as you would think of buying a business. If you can buy a business for $10 that earns $1 a year (10 PE), that would seem to be a much better value than to buy a business for $30 with that same $1 of earnings (30 PE).

So why doesn't everyone buy stocks with the lowest possible PE? Because some companies really are worth more than others. Great companies with fast earnings growth command a premium over slow-growing companies, as well they should.

To be fairly priced, a stock's PE should roughly reflect its earnings growth rate. If earnings are growing at 30 to 40 percent, then the PE should be in the 30 to 50 range. If it's growing at 15 percent per year, the PE should be closer to 15 to 20.

Selecting stocks based on PEs can be tricky. Some industries command higher PEs than others. Tobacco and military stocks, for instance, often have very low PEs, while technology and medical stocks tend to support fairly high ratios.

Perhaps the best point of comparison is the stock's own historical PEs. If a stock has had a 20 PE through most of its history, and its earnings are continuing to grow at the same pace, then you would probably be safe to buy the stock when its PE is around 20 or less. If the PE has climbed closer to 30—and the earnings growth has remained the same— you might be better served to look for other opportunities and wait for the PE of that stock to drop back down before buying.

The PE, however, is just one factor to use in judging a stock. Never buy a stock based on its PE alone. If your choice is between two excellent stocks with similar earnings growth, then it may be worthwhile to compare PEs to decide which one is truly the better bargain.

Beware the Overpriced Sector

From time to time, price-earnings ratios of an entire sector become irrationally high. If you own stocks in an overpriced sector, you can save yourself some heavy losses by unloading those stocks before they begin to plummet.

There have been several times in recent history when PEs of certain stocks became dangerously high. Those times are usually easy to recognize, because the rationale for the high prices from the experts on Wall Street is almost always the same: "This time it's different. These stocks can support exorbitantly high PEs because (fill in the blank)."

Don't believe a word of it. The decline of those stocks is imminent. Here is a brief history lesson. The most recent example was the Internet stock phenomenon. Stocks of little-known companies were carrying PEs of from 100 to 200 (and beyond). In fact, many Internet stocks had no earnings at all and no prospect for achieving earnings any time in the foreseeable future. Yet, the hype surrounding the Internet sector was so pervasive that investors poured billions of dollars into those stocks. And the higher those stocks climbed, the faster the money poured into the market. But when the bubble burst, it took down hundreds of Internet companies, along with the millions of investors who had staked much of their retirement dollars on those stocks.

But the Internet meltdown was just one in a long history of market madness. In the early 1980s, high-tech start-up stocks and biotech stocks were the rage with investors who believed that there could be no end to their spectacular growth. It mattered little that many of those companies still had no earnings, or very small earnings, and no track record. Investors still were bidding up the prices. PEs climbed into the 50 to 100 range. And the rationalizations from Wall Street's experts began: "These stocks are different from the blue chips. They can support higher PEs because of their potential for rapid growth." When the rapid growth never materialized, investors lost interest in the sector and prices fell through the floor. Stocks trading as high as $30 or $40 per share were suddenly going begging at $6 or $8.

In the late 1980s, Japanese stocks roared to record levels. Many stocks carried PEs as high as 100 to 200—levels that were virtually unheard of in the history of the stock market. Unfazed investors continued to buy, while Japanese brokers continued to tout the stocks. "This time it's different," they said. "This is the great Japanese financial empire, an empire that is taking over the world's financial markets, the world's manufacturing markets, and the world's high-technology markets. These stocks can support the higher PEs, because they are part of this great Japanese economic machine." Suddenly, the machine ground to a halt, the bottom fell out of the Japanese economy, and hundreds of stocks dropped to a fraction of their former highs. More than a decade later, Japan's Nikkei Stock Exchange was trading at about one-third of its peak level of the late 1980s.

In 1991, medical stocks suddenly caught fire. Merck climbed 80 percent. Pfizer went from $40 to $84 a share. Stryker went from $16 to $50. Across the board, medical stocks were climbing far faster than the market averages. PEs were moving into the 40 to 70 range. And once again, the rationalizations from Wall Street analysts began: "This time it's different. The world's population is aging, and the need for medical products will continue to expand. That's why these stocks can support high PEs." But in 1992, when presidential candidate Bill Clinton began talking about health care cost containment, Wall Street began to take another look at medical stocks. Suddenly, those stocks began to slide and continued to go down for about two years to the point where great stocks with great earnings such as Merck and Bristol-Myers Squibb were actually carrying PEs in the low teens. They went from overpriced to underpriced—until Wall Street finally rediscovered them in 1995 and pushed their prices back up to fair market value.

If you own stocks of a sector with PEs that seem way out of whack, be prepared to lighten your position. Your sell signal will be those wise words from Wall Street: "But this time it's different." Get out, take your profit, and move on. Invoke the Greater Fool's Theory to your own benefit and let the next guy take the fall. Or as General George Patton once put it: "The object of war is not to die for your country but to make the other bastard die for his."

Investing in Low PE Stocks

It pays to shop around in the stock market. If high PE stocks have you worried, you might consider the other extreme, low PE stocks—the stocks that no one else wants.

Some money managers specialize exclusively in low PE stocks with good success. In fact, studies have shown that low PE stocks, as a group, tend to outperform the overall market. "There is some evidence that a portfolio of stocks with relatively low earnings multiples has often produced above average rates of return," says Princeton professor Burton

Malkiel, who wrote the bestselling classic, *A Random Walk Down Wall Street.* "It has also been found that stocks that sell at low multiples of their book values have tended to produce higher subsequent returns, a finding consistent with the views that Graham and Dodd first expounded in 1934 and later championed by Warren Buffett. I would point out, however, that stocks that sell at low multiples of earnings and book values may indeed be riskier."

There's also one other problem with low PE stocks, according to money manager Lee Kopp. People who only buy low PE stocks will never own the great companies. "They're missing out on some great opportunities," says Kopp. "They have their heads in the sand." The great stocks always command a premium. You'll never see companies like General Electric and Microsoft in your broker's bargain bin.

For short-term investments, low PE stocks can provide some surprising returns. Don't build your entire portfolio around them, but if you keep an eye out for low PE stocks, you may be able to catch some big gains on the turnaround. Or as Minneapolis businessman Dennis Kleve puts it: "I'm not cheap. I just want a good deal."

Where can you find low PE stocks? Price-earnings ratios are listed in the stock tables of the *Wall Street Journal, Investor's Business Daily,* and most major newspapers. An easier way to find cheap stocks is through the *Value Line Investment Survey* (which should be available at your public library). Value Line publishes a list of the lowest PE stocks in each of its weekly updates.

A number of financial Internet sites also offer stock screening tools that will help you identify low PE stocks.

OTHER MEASURES TO CONSIDER

Although the PE is probably the most important measure of a stock's value, there are plenty of other factors to consider in judging the merits of a particular stock. Here is a laundry list of 18 factors you could examine in rating each of your stock prospects. All of the information you'll need is available at many of the leading online financial sites. I've also included a scoring system to help you rank your prospects.

1. Earnings growth past four quarters. How quickly has the company's *earnings per share* been rising over the past year. For those who wish to keep score, points should be awarded as follows: Less than 5 percent = 0 points; 5 to 9 percent = 1 point; 10 to 15 percent = 2 points; 16 to 24 percent = 3 points; 25 to 34 percent = 4 points; 35 percent and over = 5 points.

2. Earnings per share growth past five years (per year). This gives you a good indication of the company's long-term success. Scoring: Less than 10 percent per year = 0 points; 10 to 14 percent = 1 point; 15 to 19 percent = 2 points; 20 to 27 percent = 3 points; 28 to 34 percent = 4 points; 35 percent and over = 5 points.

3. Revenue growth past four quarters. This refers to growth of total sales or revenue over the past year. Points are awarded as follows: Less than 5 percent = 0 points; 5 to 9 percent = 1 point; 10 to 15 percent = 2 points; 16 to 24 percent = 3 points; 25 to 34 percent = 4 points; 35 percent and over = 5 points.

4. Revenue growth past five years (per year). This refers to growth of total sales or revenue over the most recent five-year period. Points are awarded as follows: Less than 10 percent per year = 0 points; 10 to 14 percent = 1 point; 15 to 19 percent = 2 points; 20 to 27 percent = 3 points; 28 to 34 percent = 4 points; 35 percent and over = 5 points.

5. Consistency of revenue and earnings growth. This refers to steadily rising earnings per share and revenue over the past four years. Points are awarded as follows: Four straight years of rising earnings and revenue = 5 points. One point is deducted for every time the company did not post an increase in earnings or revenue. For instance, a company with earnings gains three of the past four years and revenue gains all four years would score a 4 out of 5. A company with earnings and revenue gains three of the past four years would score just 3 out of 5. A company with earnings and revenue gains just two of the past four years would score just 1 point.

6. Growth momentum. Is the company in the midst of a solid growth spurt, or is it beginning to fade? Award points based on recent momentum of earnings and revenue growth—and projected growth.

7. Projected earnings growth next four quarters. Points are awarded based on analysts' projections of the company's earnings per share growth for the next quarter. Here is the breakdown: Less than 5 percent = 0 points; 5 to 9 percent = 1 point; 10 to 15 percent = 2 points; 16 to 24 percent = 3 points; 25 to 34 percent = 4 points; 35 percent and over = 5 points.

8. Total return past five years (per year). This refers to stock price appreciation plus dividends over the past five years, expressed as an average annual growth rate. Points are awarded as follows: Less than 10 percent = 0 points; 10 to 14 percent = 1 point; 15 to 19 percent = 2 points; 20 to 27 percent = 3 points; 28 to 34 percent = 4 points; 35 percent and over = 5 points.

9. Stock price momentum. Is the company's stock doing well in the market, or is it losing popularity? Points are awarded based on the direction and momentum of the stock price over the past several weeks and months.

10. Price-earnings ratio. Is the PE at a reasonable level? Points are awarded as follows: Under 10 = 5 points; 11 to 15 = 4 points; 16 to 24 = 3 points; 25 to 39 = 2 points; 40 to 69 = 1 point; 70 and over = 0 points.

11. Price-sales ratio. This refers to the stock price divided by the sales per share. Points are awarded as follows: Under 4 = 5 points; 4 to 6 = 4 points; 7 to 10 = 3 points; 11 to 15 = 2 points; 16 to 20 = 1 point; over 20 = 0 points.

12. Price-book ratio. This refers to the stock price divided by the book value per share of the company. (Book value per share is determined by subtracting liabilities from assets and dividing by the number of outstanding shares of stock.) Points are awarded as follows: Under

4 = 5 points; 4 to 6 = 4 points; 7 to 9 = 3 points; 10 to 13 = 2 points; 14 to 19 = 1 point; over 20 = 0 points.

13. Debt-equity ratio. This is based on long-term debt for the most recent fiscal quarter divided by total shareholder equity for the same period. Lower is better. Points are awarded as follows: Less than 0.1 = 5 points; 0.1 to 0.5 = 4 points; 0.6 to 1.0 = 3 points; 1.1 to 2.0 = 2 points; 2.1 to 4.0 = 1 point; over 4.0 = 0 points.

14. Operating margin. One measure of a company's profitability, the operating margin measures the percent of revenues remaining after paying all operating expenses. It is calculated by dividing operating income from the past four quarters by total revenue, multiplied by 100. It is expressed as a percentage. Points are awarded as follows: Under 5 percent = 0 points; 5 to 10 percent = 1 point; 11 to 19 percent = 2 points; 20 to 30 percent = 3 points; 31 to 49 percent = 4 points; 50 percent and over = 5 points. (Can be adjusted somewhat based on industry.)

15. Return on equity. Another measure of a company's profitability, the return on equity is calculated by dividing the income available to common shareholders over the past four quarters by the company's total common equity. It is expressed as a percentage. Points are awarded as follows: Under 10 percent = 0 points; 10 to15 percent = 1 point; 16 to 20 percent = 2 points; 21 to 30 percent = 3 points; 31 to 40 percent = 4 points; over 40 percent = 5 points. (Can be adjusted somewhat based on industry.)

16. Return on assets. Another measure of a company's profitability, return on assets is calculated by dividing the company's income after taxes for the past four quarters by its average total assets. It is expressed as a percentage. Points are awarded as follows: Under 1 percent = 0 points; 1 to 3 percent = 1 point; 4 to 9 percent = 2 points; 10 to 15 percent = 3 points; 16 to 29 percent = 4 points; over 30 percent = 5 points.

17. Sector strength. Score this category subjectively based on the strength of each company's industry sector.

18. Analysts' ratings. In light of the Internet stock debacle, I've developed a healthy skepticism of analysts, but their ratings may be worth a look. Do the scoring based on buy-and-sell recommendations of analysts that cover the company. Points are awarded as follows: Nearly all strong buys = 5 points; predominately strong buys and buys = 4 points; mostly buys = 3 points; mostly buys and holds = 2 points; mostly holds = 1 point; mostly holds and sells = 0 points.

DECIDING WHEN TO BUY AND SELL

Buy when the enemy is at your gate and sell the minute you hear your cavalry's bugle sounding charge.
—BARON ROTHSCHILD

There are a lot of theories floating around investment circles as to when to buy and when to sell stocks, although few are as dramatic as Baron Rothschild's gem. But there are plenty of other buy-and-sell cliches in Wall Street's trenches:

- Buy low, sell high.

- Buy on the rumor, sell on the news.

- Buy your straw hats in January and your fur coats in July.

- Buy on weakness, sell on strength.

- Buy panic, sell euphoria.

In the practical world of stock market investing, there's one system of buying stocks that seems to exceed all others because of its simplicity and success. You could call it the "no-brainer" approach, although in the business it is known as *dollar cost averaging.*

Under dollar cost averaging, you invest the same dollar amount in a stock (or a group of stocks) each month or each quarter. Dollar cost averaging relies on the volatility of the market to ensure that the investor automatically buys more shares when stocks are down and fewer shares when stocks are up.

For example, let's say that you invest $1,000 per month in GE stock. When the stock is near its high—say, $40 a share—your $1,000 contribution will buy 25 shares. But when market volatility pulls the stock down to the low end of its trading range—say, $30—your $1,000 contribution would buy about 33 shares. That's 25 shares when the stock is at the peak and 33 shares when it's at the bottom, so you automatically buy fewer shares when the market is high and more shares when it's low.

With Folio investing, you can spread your monthly (or quarterly) contribution evenly across all your holdings. In fact, you can probably make your payment automatically through a checking account deduction plan, so the process continues to work without any special effort from you. It's a no-brainer.

MORE BUY SIGNALS

We've already discussed many of the factors investors look for in making their stock selection, but let's look at a couple other investment strategies investment professionals use—momentum investing and buying on weakness.

Momentum Investing

In describing his investment philosophy, American Century Funds portfolio manager Christopher Boyd says: "The race is not always to the swift, nor the battle to the strong, but that's the way you have to bet, and that's the way we invest." Boyd loads up on stocks with rapidly growing earnings, but he is quick to dump them if the earnings growth rate declines.

"We like to find stocks that have business momentum," says Boyd. "We look for earnings and revenue acceleration. We're not as concerned about the size of the company as we are the momentum of the business. We're just trying to put the best growth companies in the portfolio." But Boyd doesn't wait for the company's annual report to see whether or not it's in a growth spurt. "By then it's too late. We look at things like orders and backlog that may have an effect on future earnings reports."

Boyd, who specializes in tech stocks and emerging growth companies, doesn't put as much weight into value measures. "We're more interested in the direction and sustainability of the growth rate than in PEs and other value factors," he explains. "But we're always aware of the PE. A high PE stock that is starting to lose growth momentum can spell trouble."

Buying on Weakness

James Crabbe is a value investor who preaches patience. "You have to sit back quietly and let the bird walk in front of you before you shoot," says Crabbe, who is the founder of the Crabbe Huson family of mutual funds. James Crabbe looks for undervalued stocks that the market has punished or forgotten. "We try to use the emotion of the market as an opportunity to buy good companies at low prices," he says. "I've seen times when a single negative earnings report would cut the price of a stock by 50 percent." Those are the stocks that grab his interest. He may not invest in every stock that takes a hit, but he will take a close look to see if there's a chance it can rebound.

"We want to see if the company has done something to correct its problems," Crabbe explains. "We're not going to invest in that stock unless we've figured out why and how the company is going to bounce back. Maybe it's new management, maybe it's a new subsidiary, maybe it's a new product, or maybe it's some cost-cutting measure. Only after we've figured that out will we buy the stock."

Although Crabbe agrees in principle with the efficient market theory (which holds that Wall Street will ultimately value every stock correctly relative to every other stock), he believes there are windows of opportunity when prices are a bit out of whack. "Over the short term, emotions can cause the stock of a good company to drop further than it should." Disappointing earnings, a failed product launch, or other bad news can cause the market to overreact. That's when Crabbe makes his move.

"It's a lot like turkey hunting," he explains. "You have to be patient." You just need to pull the trigger when the price is right.

WHEN TO SELL

Selling your winners and holding your losers is like cutting your flowers and watering your weeds.
—PETER LYNCH

Buying stocks is easy. The real science comes in deciding when—if ever—to sell.

The best time to make your sell decision is probably before you ever buy the stock. Decide then what your goals are for that stock—how high you expect it to go, how low you're willing to ride it down, how long you'll wait for the stock to move, or how high you'll ride the stock before you sell.

One of the most common mistakes made by the investing public is selling winners (for a fully taxable gain) and holding onto the losers in the hopes that those stocks will rebound. On the surface that may make sense—considering Wall Street's *buy low, sell high* mantra—but it's a strategy guaranteed to saddle you with a portfolio of losers. In order to build a portfolio of all-star stocks, you need to hold your winners and weed out your losers. Or, as they say on Wall Street: "Cut your losses and let your profits run."

That's not to say, however, that you should never sell your winners and never hold your losers. You must take it on a case-by-case basis. For instance, if one of your top stocks grows so quickly that it soon constitutes a disproportionate share of your overall portfolio, you might consider selling a few shares of the stock to give your portfolio a little better balance.

On the other hand, before you sell a falling stock, make sure there are some other compelling reasons to sell it besides a declining stock price. If the company's financial returns are starting to falter along with its stock price, that would be a good reason to dump the stock. But if the financials and future prospects remain healthy, you should probably hang onto the stock.

"We emphasize the sell side," says Jon Schoolar, a portfolio manager with the AIM family of funds. "Instead of sitting around talking about what to buy, we focus on what we should get rid of." Any stocks that show a declining earnings growth rate are quickly dropped from the fund. In examining a company's earnings, Schoolar is more concerned about the present earnings than he is past earnings or future projections. "We don't try to project earnings; we follow earnings. We also don't try to project sales of a new product. We wait and see how it does, and then we may make future sales projections based on its initial market results. We just won't buy unsubstantiated stories. We want to be able to get our hands around something we can measure."

Although growth momentum is the primary factor Schoolar looks for in evaluating a stock, he also considers the PE. "The main considera-tion with PEs is the higher the PE, the tighter our sell discipline. If a high PE stock shows any drop in momentum, we are much quicker to sell it."

Here are several other reasons to consider selling a stock.

Sell when the company no longer meets your standards. You bought a stock because the company had explosive earnings and revenue growth. Now the earnings have stopped growing, and the revenue has slowed to a trickle. That's a good reason to unload the stock. Or per-haps you bought a stock because it was the leading company in its sec-tor. Now a young upstart competitor has begun stealing market share in that sector. This may be a time to sell your stock and start buying in the other company. Or you bought a stock because its PE was especially low. Now after a run-up in the stock price, the PE doesn't seem like the bargain you once thought it was. You bought the stock because it was underpriced. Now that you've made some money and the stock is no longer underpriced, it may be the time to sell.

Sell when news is grim. If a stock you own becomes involved in a scandal, comes under legal siege, or becomes involved in a disaster, health issue, or other public controversy, take your lumps and get out as fast as you can work your keyboard. Decisive action could save you a lot of money. Take, for example, the case of Enron, the Houston-based natural gas and electricity conglomerate that was caught cooking its books. Until the scandal, Enron was the country's seventh-biggest company in terms of annual revenue. When news began to surface that Enron had helped keep billions of dollars in debt off its books through questionable partnerships, the stock was trading at around $60 a share. Over the next six months, the stock steadily dropped from $60 to $40 to $20 to $10. Finally, after the company appeared headed for bankruptcy, the stock quickly sank to under $1 a share. Investors who got out early saved thousands. Don't ride a questionable stock down. Bail quickly when news is grim.

The 20/20 rule: Sell when the stock price drops relative to the market. You might want to set up some type of safety valve for selling falling stocks. Some investors use what is known as a 10 percent/10 percent or 20 percent/20 percent rule. Here's how it works: under the 20/20 rule, you would sell the stock when it (1) drops 20 percent from its recent high and (2) drops 20 percent relative to the market. For example, if your stock drops 20 percent from $100 to $80, it meets the first criterion. But if the market also has gone down with it, then the stock still hasn't met the second criterion. If, on the other hand, the broad market has stayed the same or moved up while your stock dropped 20 percent, then it's time to sell—based on the 20/20 rule.

More aggressive investors might lean toward the more radical 10/10 rule. If your stock drops 10 percent and drops 10 percent relative to the market, sell it and move onto something more promising. The biggest problem with the 10 percent rule is that it doesn't offer much leeway. In a given year, most stocks will endure a slow period or two during which they drop 10 percent relative to the market. Most long-term-oriented investors would be better suited to the 20/20 rule.

Your own 20/20 rule. If you decide to use an automatic sell rule, like the 20/20 rule, why not tie it to your portfolio rather than a market index. If the stock drops 20 percent and 20 percent relative to your portfolio, sell a portion of your holdings in that stock—maybe 50 percent. If it keeps dropping, sell more. On the other hand, if the stock drops, but you understand why it dropped and are confident that the worst is over, you may decide not to sell at all. The sell decision is never easy.

Sell when earnings drop. Investment professionals sometimes call it the "cockroach" theory. When you see one disappointing earnings report, that may mean more bad periods loom around the corner—just as the sight of a single cockroach usually means that other bugs are hiding in the cupboards. Money managers who follow the cockroach theory like to get out of a stock at the first sign of trouble—even if it means taking a small loss to avoid taking a bigger loss later should the bad news continue. On the other hand, if it's a blue chip stock with a long history, selling after the first sign of disappointing earnings may be a mistake. If the bad news continues, don't hesitate to pull the plug. There are plenty of other promising stocks on the market for you to plug into the Folio.

The wonders of benign neglect. For many individuals, investing in stocks is a passion, a hobby, and a labor of love. Studying the market and making the tough buy-and-sell decisions is all part of the fun. But what happens if you get tired of managing your portfolio, or if you need to get away for a month or a year? Guess what? Your Folio may never miss you. In fact, sometimes it's better to step away for a while and give your stocks time to grow. A well-diversified portfolio doesn't really require constant attention. In fact, many studies have shown that more is often less—that investors and advisors who do the most trading over a given period often trail the performance of their buy-and-hold-oriented counterparts. Investing is a marathon, not a sprint. It's how you do over the long term that really matters. In the meantime, Folios give you the choice of trading aggressively or managing through benign neglect. Either method should work just fine once you've built a well-diversified portfolio of outstanding stocks.

CHAPTER 4

PRESELECTED
ALL-STAR PORTFOLIOS

T here are many ways to choose a Folio. You can pick all of the stocks yourself. You can use an index approach, buying the stocks of the Dow Jones Industrial Average. You can look up the holdings of your favorite stock mutual fund to use as a guide in building your own Folio. (Just keep in mind that the reported holdings of stock funds are often up to six months out of date.) Or you can choose from the many preselected portfolios at sites such as FOLIO*fn* and ShareBuilder.com.

In this chapter, you'll find two more ways to start a folio:

1. **15 All-Star Stock Folios.** I've put together 15 preselected Folios of promising stocks you can use as a base for your own Folios. The portfolios include blue chips, small stocks, technology stocks, medical stocks, ethical, growth and income stocks, and high-yielding stocks. (You also can find these lists—updated periodically—at <www.allstarstocks.com>.)

2. **Do-It-Yourself Blue Chip Folio Buffet.** What are the top stocks of each leading industry, based on long-term revenue and earnings growth and stock price appreciation? This guide for the do-it-yourself investor offers thumbnail sketches of the top stocks from many of the leading industries. Decide what percentage of your assets you want to put into each industrial sector, then go to the blue chip buffet to select top stocks for each of those sectors.

The stocks in both the blue chip buffet and the preselected Folios were selected based on research for my series of *100 Best Stocks* books, including *The 100 Best Stocks to Own in America, The 100 Best Stocks to Own for Under $25,* and *The 100 Best Technology Stocks for the Long Run.*

The 15 Folios include:

1. Blue Chip Diversified

2. Blue Chip Aggressive

3. Blue Chip Conservative

4. Blue Chips with Consistent Earnings Growth

5. Blue Chip Social Responsibility

6. Blue Chip Rebels without a Cause

7. High Yielding Stocks

8. Growth and Income

9. Technology Stocks Diversified

10. Technology (Computers and Communications)

11. Medical Stocks

12. Financial Stocks

13. Consumer-Oriented Stocks

14. Business-Oriented Stocks

15. Small Stocks

In narrowing down the stocks for these Folios, I looked at several factors, both tangible and intangible. Has the company posted consistent earnings and revenue growth for many years? Has the stock had solid price appreciation? Is the company a leader in its niche? Are its operations global? Does it have room to grow? Is it in an industry that's on the upswing? Is its industry cyclical or does it prosper in good times and bad?

You should consider these Folios to be merely a starting point in building your own portfolio. You may wish to add some of your own favorites and remove any stocks you think don't belong. By all means, use your own judgment. That's one of the advantages of Folios, although I can already envision the e-mails I'll be receiving. Why isn't IBM on the list? Where is Campbell's? What about Ford and GM? Please understand, these preselected Folios all feature *suggested* stocks based on my research. If there are stocks you like that are not on the list, by all means add them.

Also keep in mind that things change quickly in the investment world. Before buying any of the stocks on this list, please do some of your own research to make sure the financials are still strong and news surrounding their operations continues to be positive.

Be very selective. If you're unsure about any of the stocks on the list, move onto another stock. There are many outstanding stocks on the market. You should settle only for the ones you feel are right for you. Your right to choose, after all, is one of the primary reasons to buy Folios instead of mutual funds.

ALL-STAR STOCK FOLIOS

Most of the stocks in these preselected Folios are featured in the seventh edition of *The 100 Best Stocks to Own in America, The 100 Best Stocks to Own for Under $25,* and *The 100 Best Technology Stocks for the Long Run.* These stocks have a long history of outstanding earnings and revenue growth and are leaders in their industries.

For more information on these stocks, thumbnail descriptions are included in the "Do-It-Yourself Blue Chip Folio Buffet," which starts on page 98. (More details are also available at <www.allstarstocks.com>.)

Folio 1. Blue Chip Diversified

This is a balanced portfolio of top-rated stocks from a wide variety of industries.

Investment Companies
Alliance Capital Management (AC)
State Street Corp. (STT)
T. Rowe Price Group (TROW)

Corporate Services
Automatic Data Processing (ADP)
Cintas (CTAS)
Fiserv (FISV)
Interpublic Group (IPG)
Omnicom (OMC)
Paychex (PAYX)

Banks and Credit Institutions
Fannie Mae (FNA)
Fifth Third Bancorp (FITB)
Freddie Mac (FRE)
Household International (HI)
MBNA Corp. (KRB)
SouthTrust Corp. (SOTR)
Synovus Financial (SNV)

Medical
Abbott Labs (ABT)
Amgen (AMGN)
Johnson & Johnson (JNJ)
Medtronic (MDT)
Merck & Company (MRK)
Pfizer (PFE)
Schering-Plough (SGP)

Retail
Bed Bath & Beyond (BBBY)
Best Buy (BBY)
Home Depot (HD)

Kohl's (KSS)
Walgreen (WAG)
Wal-Mart (WMT)

Food and Beverages

Anheuser-Busch (BUD)
Coca-Cola (KO)
PepsiCo (PEP)
Safeway (SWY)
Starbucks (SBUX)
Sysco Corp. (SYY)

Miscellaneous Manufacturing

General Electric (GE)
Harley-Davidson (HDI)
United Technologies (UTX)

Technology

Cisco Systems (CSCO)
Dell Computer (DELL)
Intel (INTC)
Linear Technology (LLTC)
Microsoft (MSFT)
Oracle (ORCL)

Insurance and HMOs

AFLAC (AFL)
American International Group (AIG)
UnitedHealth Group (UNH)

Energy

ChevronTexaco (CVX)

Folio 2. Blue Chip Aggressive

This is a more aggressive portfolio, with a higher percentage of new economy stocks.

Financial
Alliance Capital Management (AC)
Fifth Third Bancorp (FITB)
T. Rowe Price Group (TROW)

Corporate Services
Cintas (CTAS)
Concord EFS (CEFT)
First Data Corp. (FDC)
Fiserv (FISV)
Paychex (PAYX)

Medical
Abbott Labs (ABT)
Amgen (AMGN)
Cardinal Health (CAH)
Genentech (DNA)
Medtronic (MDT)
Merck (MRK)
Pfizer (PFE)

Retail
Bed Bath & Beyond (BBBY)
Best Buy (BBY)
Home Depot (HD)
Kohl's (KSS)
Lowe's Companies (LOW)

Technology
AOL Time Warner (AOL)
Checkpoint Software Technology (CHKP)

Cisco Systems (CSCO)
Dell Computer (DELL)
eBay (EBAY)
EMC Corp. (EMC)
Linear Technology (LLTC)
Maxim Integrated Circuits (MXIM)
Mercury Interactive (MERQ)
Microsoft (MSFT)
Oracle (ORCL)

Miscellaneous
Donaldson Company (DCI)
Ecolab (ECL)
Harley-Davidson (HDI)

Food
Krispy Kreme Doughnuts (KKD)
Sonic Corp. (SONC)
Starbucks (SBUX)
Sysco Corp. (SYY)

Folio 3. Blue Chip Conservative

This is a more conservative portfolio, with a higher percentage of well-established companies in traditional industries, although some new economy stocks are included to provide true conservative diversification. The 50 stocks are featured in the seventh edition of *The 100 Best Stocks to Own in America*. Each has had a long history of outstanding earnings and revenue growth, and each is a leader in its respective industry. (More details also are available at <www.allstarstocks.com>.)

Banks and Credit Institutions
Fannie Mae (FNA)
Fifth Third Bancorp (FITB)
Freddie Mac (FRE)
Household International (HI)

M&T Bank (MTB)
MBNA Corp. (KRB)
SouthTrust Corp. (SOTR)
Synovus Financial (SNV)
Wells Fargo (WFI)

Consumer Products

Colgate-Palmolive (CL)
The Procter & Gamble Company (PG)

Corporate Services

Automatic Data Processing (ADP)
Cintas (CTAS)
Omnicom (OMC)

Energy

ChevronTexaco (CVX)
ExxonMobil (XOM)

Food and Beverages

Anheuser-Busch (BUD)
Coca-Cola (KO)
ConAgra (CAG)
Hershey Foods (HSY)
McDonald's (MCD)
Safeway (SWY)
Sysco Corp. (SYY)

Insurance and HMOs

AFLAC (AFL)
American International Group (AIG)
UnitedHealth Group (UNH)

Investment Companies

Alliance Capital Management (AC)
State Street Corp. (STT)

Medical
Abbott Labs (ABT)
Bristol-Myers Squibb (BMY)
Eli Lilly (LLY)
Johnson & Johnson (JNJ)
Medtronic (MDT)
Merck & Company (MRK)
Pfizer (PFE)
Schering-Plough (SGP)

Miscellaneous Manufacturing
Bemis (BMS)
Donaldson Company (DCI)
Emerson Electric (EMR)
General Electric (GE)
Tyco International (TYC)
Valspar (VAL)

Retail
Home Depot (HD)
Kohl's (KSS)
Walgreen (WAG)
Wal-Mart (WMT)

Technology
Cisco Systems (CSCO)
Dell Computer (DELL)
Intel (INTC)
Microsoft (MSFT)

Folio 4. Blue Chips with Consistent Earnings Growth

This is a portfolio of stocks that have posted more than 13 consecutive years of record earnings and revenue.

Company	Symbol	Consecutive Years of Record Earnings	Consecutive Years of Record Revenue
Automatic Data Processing	ADC	51 years	51 years
Genuine Parts	GPC	40	51
McDonald's	MCD	34	34
Cintas	CTAS	32	32
Wal-Mart	WMT	31	31
Abbott Labs	ABT	30	30
Fifth Third Bancorp	FITB	27	NA
Walgreen	WAG	26	26
Valspar	VAL	26	14
Sara Lee	SLE	26	10
State Street Corp.	STT	24	NA
Sysco Corp.	SYY	24	24
Stryker	SKY	23	23
Biomet	BMET	23	23
Sherwin-Williams	SHW	23	23
Schering-Plough	SGP	19	21
Microsoft	MFST	19	19
Interpublic Group	IPG	19	NA
Wm. Wrigley	WWY	18	18
Synovus Financial	SNV	18	NA
Bemis	BMS	16	NA
Medtronic	MDT	16	16
Fiserv	FISV	15	15
Omnicom	OMC	15	14
Fannie Mae	FNA	15	10
Johnson & Johnson	JNJ	14	25
Home Depot	HD	14	20
Donaldson Company	DCI	13	16

Folio 5. Blue Chip Social Responsibility

This is a portfolio of outstanding blue chip stocks that are also well respected for their policies on social responsibility issues.

Corporate services

Paychex (PAYX)

Financial and Insurance

AFLAC (AFL)

American International Group (AIG)

Fannie Mae (FNA)

Fifth Third Bancorp (FITB)

Freddie Mac (FRE)

State Street Corp. (STT)

Wells Fargo & Co. (WFC)

Food

H. J. Heinz (HNZ)

Sara Lee (SLE)

Maintenance Products

Ecolab (ECL)

Manufacturing

Illinois Tool Works (ITW)

Medical

Amgen (AMGN)

Johnson & Johnson (JNJ)

Medtronic (MDT)

Merck & Company (MRK)

Pfizer (PFE)

Schering-Plough (SGP)

Stryker (SYK)

Office Equipment

Pitney Bowes (PBI)

Packaging

Bemis (BMS)

Retail

Best Buy (BBY)

Home Depot (HD)
Kohl's (KSS)
Walgreen (WAG)

Consumer Products
Colgate-Palmolive (CL)

Technology
Altera (ALTR)
Cisco Systems (CSCO)
Dell Computer (DELL)
Linear Technology (LLTC)
Xilinx (XLNX)

Folio 6. Blue Chip Rebels without a Cause

This is a portfolio of stocks often excluded by socially responsible funds. If you feel no ill will toward aerospace and defense contractors, companies that produce tobacco or alcoholic beverages, companies that harvest natural resources such as lumber or oil, or companies that produce chemicals, plastics, or oil-based products that could affect the environment, you may find this list helpful. Pick and choose the ones that may be right for you.

Defense
Alliant Techsystems (ATK) Aerospace, weapons, and ammunition
Boeing (BA) Commercial and military aircraft
General Dynamics (GD) Tanks, submarines, and other weapons and ammunition
General Electric (GE) Aerospace equipment
Kaman (KAMN A) Helicopters and other aerospace equipment
Lockheed-Martin (LMT) Space and missile systems, aeronautics, and information systems
Mercury Computer Systems (MRCY) Computer imaging systems that see behind enemy lines

Raytheon (RTNA) Air defense systems, missiles, radar, and other military systems

United Technologies (UTX) Aircraft engines and flight systems

Energy

BP PLC (formerly British Petroleum and Amoco) (BP)

ChevronTexaco (CVX)

ExxonMobil (XOM)

Kinder Morgan, Inc. (KMI) Natural gas

Chemicals, Coatings, and Plastics

Rohm & Haas (ROH) Specialty chemicals, plastics, additives, coatings, and adhesives

RPM (RPM) Paints and coatings

Sherwin-Williams (SHW) Paints and coatings

Sigma-Aldrich (SIAL) Specialty chemicals, biochemicals, and organic chemicals

Valspar (VAL) Paints and coatings

Paper Products

Kimberly-Clark (KMB) Paper products

Alcohol and Tobacco

Anheuser-Busch (BUD) World's largest beer producer

Philip Morris (MO) (Soon to be Altria Group) World's largest cigarette producer

RJ Reynolds Tobacco (RJR) Cigarettes

UST (UST) Chewing tobacco

Folio 7. High Yielding Stocks

This portfolio is appropriate for investors who are more interested in income than stock price appreciation. The 40 stocks on this list all pay dividends that rank among the highest in the stock market. However, stock price appreciation is not necessarily a strong point for many of these companies. Many are utility companies that have had only modest price appreciation in recent years. For those investors seeking income, the dividends paid by these stocks dramatically exceeds the yield you would receive from most bank accounts and certificates of deposit. The stocks are listed by industry group.

Investment Companies

Company	Symbol	Recent Dividend Yield
Alliance Capital Management	AC	6%
ACM Income Fund	ACG	11
Duff & Phelps	DNP	7
J. Hancock Patriot Prem. Div. Fund	PDF	7
MFS Multimarket Income Fund	MMT	7
Scudder High Income Trust	KHI	11

Real Estate Investment Trusts (REITs)

Company	Symbol	Recent Dividend Yield
Archstone-Smith Trust	ASN	6 %
BRE Properties	BRE	6
Duke Realty	DRE	6
Equity Residential	EQR	6
Health Care Property	HCP	9
Penn REIT	PEI	8
Simon Property GP	SPG	7
United Dominion Trust	UDR	7
Weingarten Realty	WRI	6.5

Insurance (Property & Casualty)

Company	Symbol	Recent Dividend Yield
American Financial Group	AFG	4%

Natural Gas Diversified

Company	Symbol	Recent Dividend Yield
Kinder Morgan Energy Partners	KMP	6 %
Teppco Partners	TPP	7.5

Electric Utilities (West)

Company	Symbol	Recent Dividend Yield
Hawaiian Electric	HE	6 %
Puget Energy	PSD	8.5
Sempra Energy	SRE	4
XCEL Energy	XEL	5

Electric Utilities (Central)

Company	Symbol	Recent Dividend Yield
Allete	ALE	4 %
Alliant Energy	LNT	6.5
Ameren	AEE	6
American Electric Power	AEP	5.5
Cinergy	CIN	5
DTE Energy Co.	DTE	5
Empire District	EDE	6
OGE Energy	OGE	6
Reliant Energy	REI	5.5
TXU Corp.	TXU	5
WPS Resources	WPS	6

Electric Utilities (East)

Company	Symbol	Recent Dividend Yield
Allegheny Energy	AYE	5 %
American Electric Power	AEP	5.5
Con Edison	ED	5
PPL Corp.	PPL	3
PS Enterprise Group	PEG	5
RGS Energy Group	RGS	5
UIL Holdings	UIL	6

Folio 8. Growth and Income

This portfolio is appropriate for investors who are interested in both income and stock price appreciation. The stocks on this list pay solid dividends, and many have posted fairly solid revenue, earnings, and stock price growth over the past few years. Although there may be many other stocks on the market with better growth records, these stocks provide a combination of both dividend income and promising growth potential.

Company	Symbol	Recent Dividend Yield
ABM Ind.	ABM	2 %
Alliance Capital	AC	6
Alliant Energy	LNT	6.5
American Water Works	AWK	2
AmSouth Bancorp	ASO	5
Avery Dennison	AVY	2
BB&T	BBT	3
Bank One	ONE	2
Bemis	BMS	2
Caterpillar	CAT	3
ChevronTexaco	CVX	3
ConAgra	CAG	4
ExxonMobil	XOM	2
Heinz	HNZ	4
Hershey Foods	HSY	2
Hubbell	HUBB	4
International Aluminum	IAL	5
Kellogg	K	3
Lance	LNCE	4
May Dept. Stores	MAY	2.5
Nash-Finch	NAFC	1
PACCAR	PCAR	2
Peoples Bank	PBCT	6
Pitney Bowes	PBI	3
Plum Creek Timber	PCL	8
RPM	RPM	3
Sara Lee	SLE	3
Sherwin-Williams	SHW	2
SouthTrust	SOTR	2
SunTrust	STI	2.5
Tasty Baking	TBC	3
WD 40	WDFC	4

Folio 9. Technology Stocks Diversified

This is a portfolio of 45 stocks from a broad range of technology sectors, including computers, communications, biotechnology, medical technology, software, energy, the Internet, and technology services. The stocks listed here are featured in *The 100 Best Technology Stocks for the Long Run.* Although the economic slowdown has been a drag on all technology companies, the ones listed here have held up better than most and are leaders in their respective industry sectors. For more information on these stocks, thumbnail descriptions are included in the "Do-It-Yourself Blue Chip Folio Buffet," which starts on page 98. (More details also are available at <www.allstarstocks.com>.)

Biotech and Medical Technology
Affymetrix (AFFX)
Amgen (AMGN)
Applied Biosystems Group (ABI)
Biogen (BGEN)
Genentech (DNA)
Medimmune (MEDI)
Medtronic (MDT)

Computers and Peripherals
Dell Computer (DELL)
EMC (EMC)
International Business Machines (IBM)
Mercury Computer Systems (MRCY)
Sun Microsystems (SUNW)
Tech Data Corp. (TECD)

Business Services and Outsourcing
Celestica (CLS)
Flextronics International (FLEX)
InterCept Group (ICPT)

E-commerce
Amazon.com (AMZN)
AOL Time Warner (AOL)
eBay (EBAY)
Yahoo! (YHOO)

Energy
AstroPower (APWR)

General
General Electric (GE)
United Technologies (UTX)

Internet Infrastructure
CheckPoint Software Technology (CHKP)
Cisco Systems (CSCO)
Juniper Networks (JNPR)
Mercury Interactive (MERQ)
VeriSign (VRSN)

Semiconductors
Altera (ALTR)
Analog Devices (ADI)
Applied Materials (AMAT)
Intel (INTC)
Linear Technology (LLTC)
Microchip Technology (MCHP)
Maxim Integrated Products (MXIM)
NVIDIA (NVDA)
Xilinx (XLNX)

Software
Citrix Systems (CTXS)
Electronic Arts (ERTS)
Microsoft (MSFT)

Oracle (ORCL)
Veritas Software (VRTS)

Telecommunications
Nokia (NOK)
Verizon Communications (VZ)
Viasat (VSAT)

Folio 10. Technology (Computers and Communications)

This is a portfolio of 41 stocks from the computer and communications sectors, including computers, telecommunications, software, the Internet, and technology services. Although the economic slowdown has been a drag on all technology companies, the ones listed here have held up better than most and are leaders in their respective industry sectors.

Computers and Peripherals
Advanced Digital Information Corp. (ADIC)
Dell Computer (DELL)
EMC (EMC)
International Business Machines (IBM)
Mercury Computer Systems (MRCY)
Sun Microsystems (SUNW)
Tech Data Corp. (TECD)

Business Services and Outsourcing
Celestica (CLS)
Flextronics International (FLEX)
InterCept Group (ICPT)

E-commerce
Amazon.com (AMZN)
AOL Time Warner (AOL)
eBay (EBAY)
Yahoo! (YHOO)

Internet Infrastructure

CheckPoint Software Technology (CHKP)
Cisco Systems (CSCO)
Internet Security Systems (ISSX)
Juniper Networks (JNPR)
Mercury Interactive (MERQ)
VeriSign (VRSN)

Semiconductors

Altera (ALTR)
Analog Devices (ADI)
Applied Materials (AMAT)
Broadcom (BRCM)
Intel (INTC)
Linear Technology (LLTC)
Microchip Technology (MCHP)
Maxim Integrated Products (MXIM)
NVIDIA (NVDA)
Xilinx (XLNX)

Software

Avant! (AVNT)
Citrix Systems (CTXS)
Electronic Arts (ERTS)
Microsoft (MSFT)
Oracle (ORCL)
SunGard Data Systems (SDS)
Veritas Software (VRTS)

Telecommunications

Nokia (NOK)
Polycom (PLCM)
Vodafone Group PLC (VOD)
Viasat (VSAT)

Folio 11. Medical Stocks

This is a portfolio of 30 medical-related stocks, including pharmaceutical makers, medical technology companies, biotech firms, service providers, and related sectors.

Biotechnology
Affymetrix (AFFX)
Amgen (AMGN)
Applied Biosystems Group (ABI)
Biogen (BGEN)
Genentech (DNA)
Medimmune (MEDI)

Distribution
Cardinal Health (CAH)

Medical-Agricultural
Embrex (EMBX)

Medical Products
Abbott Laboratories (ABT)
Biomet (BMET)
Exactech (EXAC)
Kensey Nash Corp. (KNSY)
Stryker (SYK)

Medical Services
AmeriPath, Inc. (PATH)
AmSurg Corp. (AMSG)
UnitedHealth (UHN)
Universal Health Services (UHS)

Medical Technology
Guidant (GDT)
Medtronic (MDT)

Pharmaceuticals and Consumer Products

American Home Products (AHP)
Bristol-Myers Squibb (BMY)
Colgate-Palmolive (CL)
Forest Laboratories (FRX)
Johnson & Johnson (JNJ)
Eli Lilly (LLY)
Merck & Co. (MRK)
North American Scientific, Inc. (NASI)
Pfizer (PFE)
Schering-Plough (SGP)
Taro Pharmaceuticals Industries (TARO)

Folio 12. Financial Stocks

This is a portfolio of 25 financial-related stocks, including investment companies, banks, insurance firms, and credit firms.

Banking and Lending

BB&T (BBT)
Fannie Mae (FNA)
Fifth Third Bancorp (FITB)
Freddie Mac (FRE)
M&T Bank (MTB)
PFF Bancorp, Inc. (PFFB)
SouthTrust Corp. (SOTR)
SunTrust Corp. (STI)
Synovus Financial (SNV)
US Bancorp (USB)
Wells Fargo (WFI)

Credit-Related Companies

Household International (HI)
MBNA Corp. (KRB)

Insurance and HMOs
AFLAC (AFL)
American International Group (AIG)
Jefferson-Pilot (JP)
Protective Life (PL)
UnitedHealth Group (UNH)

Investment Companies
Alliance Capital Management (AC)
Franklin Resources (BEN)
Legg Mason (LM)
State Street Corp. (STT)
T. Rowe Price (TROW)

Services
Actrade International, Ltd. (ACRT)
Fiserv (FISV)

Folio 13. Consumer-Oriented Stocks

This is a portfolio of 30 consumer-oriented stocks, including food and beverage companies, retailers, restaurants, consumer services firms, and other consumer products makers.

Apparel
Jones Apparel Group (JNY)
Nike (NKE)

Entertainment
AOL Time Warner (AOL)

Food and Beverages
Anheuser-Busch (BUD)
Coca-Cola (KO)
ConAgra (CAG)
Hershey Foods

PepsiCo (PEP)
Sara Lee (SLE)
Sysco Corp. (SYY)
William Wrigley (WWY)

Food and Drug Retail
Kroger (KR)
Safeway (SWY)
Walgreen (WAG)

General Consumer Products
Colgate-Palmolive (CP)
Procter & Gamble (PG)
Sherwin-Williams (SHW)
Valspar (VAL)

Home Construction
Toll Brothers (TOL)

Restaurants
McDonald's (MCD)
Sonic (SONC)
Starbucks (SBUX)

Retail
Abercrombie & Fitch (ANF)
Bed Bath & Beyond (BBBY)
Best Buy (BBY)
Home Depot (HD)
Kohl's (KSS)
Wal-Mart (WMT)

Transportation
Harley-Davidson (HDI)
Southwest Airlines (LUV)

Folio 14. Business-Oriented Stocks

This is a portfolio of 20 business-oriented stocks, including advertising, business services, equipment and supplies, and outsourcing.

Advertising
Interpublic Group (IPG)
Omnicom (OMC)

Business Services
ABM Industries (ABM)
Concord EFS (CEFT)
Equifax (EFX)
InterCept Group (ICPT)
First Data (FDC)
Fiserv (FISV)

Equipment and Supplies
Avery Dennison (AVY)
Cintas (CTAS)
Dionex (DNEX)
Fastenal (FAST)
Herman Miller (MLHR)
Pitney Bowes (PBI)
Tyco International (TYC)

Outsourcing
Cambrex (CBM)
Celestica (CLS)
Flextronics International (FLEX)

Payroll Services
Automatic Data Processing (ADP)
Paychex (PAYX)

Folio 15. Small Stocks

This small stock portfolio is for aggressive investors or those who wish to bring greater diversification to their holdings by adding a small stock position to a broader diversified portfolio of blue chip stocks. Most of the stocks on this list are featured in *The 100 Best Stocks to Own for Under $25* and have established a solid track record of earnings and revenue growth. (More details on investing in this Folio also are available at <www.allstarstocks.com>.)

Automotive
Sonic Automotive, Inc. (SAH)

Business Services
Actrade International (ACRT)

Communications
Gentner Communications (GTNR)
SpectraLink Corp. (SLNK)

Computer
Networking
Quality Systems, Inc. (QSII)
Trend Micro, Inc. (TMIC)

Products
Advanced Digital Information Corp. (ADIC)
Drexler Technology Corp. (DRXR)

Semiconductors
Amtech Systems, Inc. (ASYS)
ESS Technology, Inc. (ESST)
Genesis Microchip, Inc. (GNSS)
Semitool, Inc. (SMTL)
Xicor, Inc. (XICO)

Services
InterCept Group, Inc. (ICPT)

Software
Avant! Corp. (AVNT)
Integral Systems, Inc. (ISYS)
Mechanical Dynamics, Inc. (MDII)
Novadigm, Inc. (NVDM)

Energy
Astro Power, Inc. (APWR)

Financial
PFF Bancorp, Inc. (PFFB)

Manufacturing
CompuDyne Corp. (CDCY)
Concord Camera Corp. (LENS)

Medical Products
Embrex, Inc. (EMBX)
Exactech, Inc. (EXAC)
Kensey Nash Corp. (KNSY)
North American Scientific, Inc. (NASI)

Medical Services
AmeriPath, Inc. (PATH)
AmSurg Corp. (AMSG)

Pharmaceuticals
Axcan Pharma, Inc. (AXCA)
Taro Pharmaceuticals Industries Ltd. (TARO)

Retail and Restaurants
Abercrombie & Fitch Co. (ANF)
Sonic (SONC)

DO-IT-YOURSELF BLUE CHIP FOLIO BUFFET

Build your own Folio of outstanding blue chip stocks. This guide for the do-it-yourself investor offers thumbnail sketches of some of the top performing stocks from a wide range of industries. Decide what percentage of your assets you want to put into each industrial sector, then review the selections in the Blue Chip Buffet to determine the specific stocks you want to buy. The stocks are grouped by industrial sector.

These stocks are featured in the seventh edition of *The 100 Best Stocks to Own in America, The 100 Best Stocks to Own for Under $25,* and *The 100 Best Technology Stocks for the Long Run.* Each stock has had a solid history of earnings and revenue growth, and each is a leader in its respective industry. (For more information, consult the books listed above or visit my Web site, <www.allstarstocks.com>.)

The industrial sectors represented include:

- Banking and Lending

- Business Services and Outsourcing

- Chemicals, Coatings, and Cleansers

- Computer Technology (computers and related products, semiconductors, software, Internet infrastructure, and e-commerce)

- Construction

- Consumer Products

- Electronics and Electrical Products

- Energy

- Entertainment

- Food and Beverages

- Food and Drug Retail

- Medical (biotechnology, pharmaceuticals and medical products, and health care services)

- Industrial Equipment and Supplies

- Insurance and HMOs

- Investing and Financial

- Office Equipment and Supplies

- Packaging

- Restaurants

- Retail

- Telecommunications

- Transportation

BANKING AND LENDING

BB&T Corporation
200 West Second Street
Winston-Salem, NC 27101
336-733-2000
NYSE: BBT
www.bbandt.com

BB&T (formerly Branch Banking and Trust) has used a corporate buying binge the past ten years to transform itself from a small regional bank to one of the larger financial services companies in the southeastern United States. The Winston-Salem, North Carolina, institution has acquired more than 50 banks and thrifts, 47 insurance agencies, and 14 financial service providers over the past decade. BB&T has about 930 branch offices in the Southeast. Founded in 1872, BB&T is the oldest bank headquartered in North Carolina. The company has about 17,500 employees and a market capitalization of about $15 billion.

Fannie Mae

3900 Wisconsin Avenue
Washington, DC 20016
202-752-7115
NYSE: FNM
www.fanniemae.com

Fannie Mae (the Federal National Mortgage Association) has helped more than 30 million American families put a permanent roof over their heads. The Washington, D.C.–based operation is the nation's largest provider of residential mortgage funding. The company buys mortgages from lenders, such as banks, mortgage banks, and savings and loan associations, thereby replenishing their funds for additional lending. The company has posted 14 consecutive years of record earnings. Fannie Mae has about 3,200 employees and 240,000 shareholders and has a market capitalization of about $80 billion.

Fifth Third Bancorp

Fifth Third Center
38 Fountain Square Plaza
Cincinnati, OH 45263
513-579-5300
Nasdaq: FITB
www.53.com

For more than a quarter century, an investment in Fifth Third Bancorp has been like money in the bank—only better. The Cincinnati-based banking organization has posted 27 consecutive years of record earnings and revenue—the most consistent banking organization in America. With its recent acquisition of Old Kent, the 143-year-old Cincinnati institution has grown to about 1,000 branch offices throughout Ohio, Michigan, Kentucky, Indiana, Florida, and Arizona. Fifth Third has about 12,000 employees and 38,000 shareholders and has a market capitalization of about $22 billion.

Freddie Mac
8200 Jones Branch Drive
McLean, VA 22102
703-903-3725
NYSE: FRE
www.freddiemac.com

Over the past 31 years, Freddie Mac (the Federal Home Loan Mortgage Corporation) has financed the purchase of one out of every six homes in America. Established by Congress in 1970, Freddie Mac provides a continuous flow of funds for residential mortgages by buying mortgage loans and mortgage-related securities in the secondary market. Freddie Mac has about 3,200 employees and a market capitalization of about $45 billion.

Household International, Inc.
2700 Sanders Road
Prospect Heights, IL 60070
847-205-7490
NYSE: HI
www.household.com

Household International has become one of the nation's leading lenders by targeting the customers no one else wants. The company's prime targets are consumers who have limited credit histories, modest incomes, high debt-to-income ratios, or previous credit problems. Household can charge a higher interest rate to those customers to compensate for the additional risk. Household operates 1,400 branch offices in 46 states and claims about 3.5 million customers. The branches are operated under the company's subsidiaries—HFC and Beneficial Finance. Founded in 1878, Household has about 29,000 employees and a market capitalization of about $32 billion.

MBNA Corporation
1100 North King Street
Wilmington, DE 19884
800-362-6255
NYSE: KRB
www.MBNA.com

MBNA has become the world's leading independent credit card lender
through an aggressive mass mailing and telemarketing campaign. MBNA
is the leading issuer of "affinity credit cards," which are specially designed cards endorsed by organizations, universities, associations, and
other groups. The company has about 23,000 employees and 2,800
shareholders and has a market capitalization of about $8 billion.

M&T Bank Corporation
One M&T Plaza
Buffalo, NY 14203
716-842-5445
NYSE: MTB
www.mandtbank.com

Founded more than 140 years ago, the M&T Bank Corporation (formerly known as First Empire State Corp.) has been growing rapidly
through a series of acquisitions. The company has about 500 branch offices throughout New York, Pennsylvania, Maryland, and West Vir-
ginia. M&T Bank has about 9,000 employees and 5,000 shareholders
and has a market capitalization of about $7 billion.

SouthTrust Corporation
420 North 20th Street
Birmingham, AL 35203
205-254-5530
Nasdaq: SOTR
www.southtrust.com

A prudent loan policy and a voracious appetite for acquisitions have helped make SouthTrust Corporation one of the fastest growing banking organizations in the country. The Birmingham-based operation has more than 650 banking offices and several bank-related affiliates throughout the South. The company has about 12,000 employees and 14,000 shareholders of record and has a market capitalization of about $8 billion.

SunTrust Banks, Inc.

303 Peachtree Street, N.E.
Atlanta, GA 30308
404-588-7711
NYSE: STI
www.suntrust.com

SunTrust branches are spread far and wide across the sun-drenched cities of the southeastern United States. The Atlanta institution operates more than 1,100 branches in the Southeast and a network of nearly 2,000 ATM machines. SunTrust has about 30,000 employees and a market capitalization of about $18 billion.

Synovus Financial Corporation

901 Front Avenue, Suite 120
P.O. Box 120
Columbus, GA 31902
706-649-2311
NYSE: SNV
www.synovus.com

If you live in the South, you may be a Synovus Financial customer without even knowing it. The Columbus, Georgia banking institution owns 39 separate banks—with more than 200 locations—all under different names. The company has become one of the biggest banking organizations in the South through a steady series of acquisitions. Founded in

1887, Synovus has about 10,000 employees and 16,000 shareholders and has a market capitalization of about $9 billion.

U.S. Bancorp

601 Second Avenue South
Minneapolis, MN 55402
612-973-1111
NYSE: USB
www.usbancorp.com

When U.S. Bancorp merged with Firstar Bank in 2001, the combined operation was suddenly one of the biggest banks in the United States—particularly in the West and Midwest. The company has about 10 million customers in 24 midwestern and western states. It has more than 2,300 banking and retail brokerage offices and a network of more than 5,000 ATMs. The combined banking operation has about 53,000 employees and a market capitalization of about $20 billion.

Wells Fargo & Company

420 Montgomery Street
San Francisco, CA 94163
800-411-4932
NYSE: WFC
www.wellsfargo.com

Wells Fargo doesn't do business out of a stagecoach anymore. It has 5,500 shiny branch stores for its banking customers to use. The San Francisco–based operation is now the fourth largest bank in America, thanks to its 1998 merger with Norwest Corp. Wells Fargo has about 113,000 employees and 50,000 shareholders and has a market capitalization of about $83 billion.

BUSINESS SERVICES AND OUTSOURCING

ABM Industries
160 Pacific Avenue, Suite 222
San Francisco, CA 94111
415-733-4000
NYSE: ABM
www.abm.com

ABM Industries does the dirty work of thousands of corporations and institutions across North America. The company is one of the largest facility services contractors in the country, with annual revenues of nearly $2 billion. Building maintenance is ABM's biggest area. Founded in 1909, the company has about 60,000 employees and a market capitalization of about $800 million.

Automatic Data Processing, Inc.
One ADP Boulevard
Roseland, NJ 07068
973-974-5000
NYSE: ADP
www.adp.com

Automatic Data Processing (ADP) cuts the checks for more than 29 million workers a week. The company is the leading provider of payroll and tax filing processing, offering transaction processing, data communications, and information services for about 500,000 corporate clients. In terms of earnings growth, ADP has been the most consistent company in America. Since it opened in 1949, the Roseland, New Jersey operation has posted record sales and earnings for 51 consecutive years. ADP has 40,000 employees and about 25,000 shareholders and has a market capitalization of about $35 billion.

Celestica, Inc.
844 Don Mills Road
Ontario, M3C 1V7
Toronto, Canada
416-448-5800
NYSE: CLS
www.celestica.com

Celestica's earthly mission is to do the heavy lifting for the world's leading electronics manufacturers. It's an unheralded mission, because none of the PCs, workstations, servers, printed circuit assemblies, or networking equipment produced at its 36 plants around the world bears the Celestica name. The outsourcing specialist is the third-largest electronics manufacturer services, or EMS, company in the world. Celestica has about 14,000 employees.

Cintas Corporation
6800 Cintas Boulevard
P.O. Box 65737
Cincinnati, OH 45262
513-459-1200
Nasdaq: CTAS
www.cintas-corp.com

Four million Americans wear a Cintas uniform to work each day. The Cincinnati operation is the nation's largest provider of corporate uniforms, supplying the clothing for a wide range of businesses, from delivery services and airlines to service stations and retail chains. Cintas has posted 32 consecutive years of record sales and earnings. Founded in 1968, Cintas has 22,500 employees, 26,000 shareholders, and a market capitalization of about $8 billion.

Concord EFS, Inc.

2525 Horizon Lake Drive, Suite 120

Memphis, TN 38133

901-371-8000

Nasdaq: CEFT

www.concordefs.com

Concord EFS helps retailers take your money. It is the leading player in the merchant card electronic transaction processing business. Through all of its divisions, Concord is involved in 50 percent of all ATM debit transactions and 60 percent of all point-of-sale debit transactions in the United States, providing electronic transaction processing services to restaurants, financial institutions, supermarkets, service stations, convenience stores, and other independent retailers. Founded in 1970, Concord EFS has about 2,000 employees and a market capitalization of about $12 billion.

Equifax, Inc.

15500 Peachtree Street, N.W.

Atlanta, GA 30309

404-885-8000

NYSE: EFX

www.equifax.com

Equifax makes *your* business *its* business. The Atlanta-based operation is the nation's largest credit reporting operation, providing consumer credit reports for banks, retailers, financial institutions, utilities, oil companies, credit card companies, automobile finance and leasing firms, and mortgage lenders. The company has about 12,000 employees and 11,000 shareholders and has a market capitalization of $5 billion.

First Data Corporation
6200 South Quebec Street
Greenwood, CO 80111
303-488-8000
NYSE: FDC
www.firstdata.com

First Data helps retailers collect from their customers. It is the leading electronic commerce and payment services company in the world, with a customer base that includes nearly 3 million merchant locations and 1,400 credit card issuers. It is the parent company of Western Union, which is the world leader in money transfers and money orders. First Data has about 25,000 employees and a market capitalization of about $26 billion.

Fiserv, Inc.
255 Fiserv Drive
Brookfield, WI 53054
262-879-5000
Nasdaq: FISV
www.fiserv.com

Fiserv helps bankers keep track of their money. The Milwaukee-area operation is the nation's largest data processing provider for banks and savings institutions. The company provides a wide range of data processing services for nearly 8,000 financial clients. Fiserv has about 14,000 employees, 20,000 shareholders, and a market capitalization of about $7 billion.

Flextronics International
11 Ubi Road I #07-01/02
Meiban Industrial Building
Singapore 408723, Singapore
408-383-7722

Nasdaq: FLEX
www.flextronics.com

Want something done right? Get someone else to do it. That's what Flextronics has persuaded dozens of telecommunications, computer, networking, and electronics companies to do. The Singapore-based operation is the world's third largest electronics manufacturing services operation. Flextronics does the manufacturing of hundreds of products for such leading technology companies as Cisco, Ericsson, Hewlett-Packard, Lucent, Microsoft, Motorola, and Nokia. Flextronics has about 37,000 employees.

The InterCept Group, Inc.

3150 Holcomb Bridge Road, Suite 200
Norcross, GA 30071
770-248-9600
Nasdaq: ICPT
www.tellerplus.com

Small community banks can use the same type of electronic transaction processes as the big institutions thanks to a comprehensive line of banking software offered by the InterCept Group. InterCept provides software and services for electronic funds transfer services, data communication management, check imaging, Internet banking, client-server enterprise software, and other processing solutions for more than 1,400 community banks and savings institutions. The company has about 320 employees.

Interpublic Group of Companies

1271 Avenue of the Americas
New York, NY 10020
212-399-8000
NYSE: IPG
www.interpublic.com

For the past century, Interpublic Group has been pushing products and polishing images the world over. Founded in 1902, Interpublic has more than 40 agencies and related divisions and represents such world-class operations as Coca-Cola, Unilever, Nestlé, and Chevrolet. It is the world's second largest advertising group. The New York–based agency has about 48,000 employees, 3,500 shareholders, and a market capitalization of about $12 billion.

Omnicom Group, Inc.

437 Madison Avenue
New York, NY 10022
212-415-3600
NYSE: OMC
www.omnicomgroup.com

Talk about your World Wide Web. Omnicom, the global advertising conglomerate, operates more than 1,400 separate companies, with customers in more than 100 countries. The Madison Avenue agency is responsible for some of America's leading ad campaigns, such as "Got Milk" and Budweiser's "Louie the Lizard." The crown jewel of the Omnicom empire is BBDO Worldwide. Omnicom has 56,000 employees, 4,200 shareholders, and a market capitalization of about $17 billion.

Paychex, Inc.

911 Panorama Trail South
Rochester, NY 14625
716-385-6666
Nasdaq: PAYX
www.paychex.com

Paychex processes the payroll checks for more than 350,000 companies. As the nation's second largest payroll services company, Paychex cuts the checks for more than 4 million workers nationwide—133 million paychecks a year. The firm works primarily with small to midsized companies. The company has about 6,000 employees, 4,000 share-holders, and a market capitalization of about $15 billion.

Sanmina Corporation
2700 North First Street
San Jose, CA 95134
408-964-3500
Nasdaq: SANM
www.sanmina.com

In the fast-paced world of high technology, time to market has become increasingly important. That's one reason why electronics manufacturers are turning increasingly to high-tech specialty firms such as San-mina to manufacture the sophisticated components inside their products. Sanmina specializes in custom-manufacturing printed circuit boards and related items used in a variety of electronic devices such as computers, telephones, and medical equipment. The company has about 24,000 employees.

CHEMICALS, COATINGS, AND CLEANSERS

Cambrex Corporation
One Meadowlands Plaza
East Rutherford, NJ 07073
201-804-3000
Nasdaq: CBM
www.cambrex.com

Cambrex provides the building blocks for the next generation of mira-cle drugs. The company offers pharmaceutical outsourcing services for both biological and chemical platforms, including tools for DNA and protein separation and sequencing, cell-based bioassays, and a broad line of human cells, including adult stem cells. Founded in 1981, Cambrex has about 2,000 employees and 4,400 shareholders and has a market capitalization of about $1.5 billion.

Ecolab, Inc.
370 N. Wabasha Street
St. Paul, MN 55102
651-293-2233
NYSE: ECL
www.ecolab.com

Ecolab may not scrub behind your ears, but the company offers a broad range of cleaning and sanitizing products that help keep the world cleaner, fresher, and more sanitary. Ecolab is one of the world's leading manufacturers of maintenance products and services for the hospitality, institutional, and industrial markets. Founded in 1923, Ecolab has about 13,000 employees and 6,000 shareholders and has a market capitalization of about $5 billion.

Sherwin-Williams Company
101 Prospect Avenue N.W.
Cleveland, OH 44115
216-566-2000
NYSE: SHW
www.sherwin.com

Known for its all-weather paints, Sherwin-Williams has been an all-weather kind of company. Earnings growth has slowed recently, but the Cleveland-based operation has still managed to post record earnings for 23 consecutive years. Sherwin-Williams is the nation's largest producer of paints and varnishes. It has about 2,300 paint stores in the United States and operations in about 30 other countries. Founded in 1866, Sherwin-Williams has about 26,000 employees, 12,000 shareholders, and a market capitalization of about $4 billion.

Sigma-Aldrich Corporation

3050 Spruce Street
St. Louis, MO 63103
314-771-5765
Nasdaq: SIAL
www.sigma-aldrich.com

Sigma-Aldrich keeps the world's research laboratories well stocked with biochemical and organic chemical products. The company supplies more than 80,000 chemicals used in scientific and genomic research, biotechnology, pharmaceutical development, chemical manufacturing, and medical diagnosis. It is the world's leading supplier of research chemicals and products used in life-science and high-tech applications. It has about 6,100 employees and a market capitalization of about $3.2 billion.

Valspar Corporation

1101 Third Street South
Minneapolis, MN 55415
612-332-7371
NYSE: VAL
www.valspar.com

Valspar makes red paint in many shades, but the company has been careful not to spill any on the corporate balance sheet. Paint it black, in fact, with 26 consecutive years of record earnings. Valspar paints have been a mainstay of the American landscape for nearly 200 years. The company has 4,500 employees, 1,900 shareholders, and a market capitalization of about $1.5 billion.

COMPUTER TECHNOLOGY

Computers and Related Products

Advanced Digital Information Corporation

11431 Willows Road N.E.

P.O. Box 97057

Redmond, WA 98073

425-881-8004

Nasdaq: ADIC

www.advanceddigital.com

The ongoing quest for bigger computer systems, more complex software, and larger Web sites has cranked up the need for computer data storage space. Advanced Digital Information Corporation (ADIC) has developed a line of high-capacity data storage devices to cash in on that growing demand. Founded in 1983, ADIC has about 800 employees and a market capitalization of about $800 million.

Brocade Communications

1745 Technology Drive

San Jose, CA 95110

408-487-8000

Nasdaq: BRCD

www.brocade.com

Data storage has become big business with the advent of the Internet and massive corporate computer networks. Brocade is a leading maker of switching systems designed to facilitate the use of large storage area networks (SANs). The company, which has about 600 employees, made its initial public stock offering in 1999. It has a market capitalization of about $5 billion.

Dell Computer Corporation

One Dell Way
Round Rock, TX 78682
512-338-4400
Nasdaq: DELL
www.dell.com

Dell has made its mark in the computer industry by going directly to the consumer. In fact, it has become the world's largest direct seller of computer systems. Dell Computer founder Michael Dell built his business on the direct marketing approach, which cuts costs by eliminating the markups that would otherwise go to the wholesale and retail dealers. Founded in 1984, Dell has about 40,000 employees and a market capitalization of about $55 billion.

EMC Corporation

35 Parkwood Drive
Hopkinton, MA 01748
508-435-1000
NYSE: EMC
www.emc.com

As corporations and institutions expand their computer networks, adding e-mail, e-commerce, voice, video, and graphics applications, they soon find themselves running short of digital storage space. EMC helps solve the storage shortage by offering a line of high-capacity digital storage systems. It is the market leader in the enterprise data storage market, with more than a 50 percent share of the mainframe storage market. EMC has about 24,000 employees and a market capitalization of about $35 million.

International Business Machines
One New Orchard Road
Armonk, NY 10504
914-499-1900
NYSE: IBM
www.ibm.com

IBM was once the clear leader in the computer technology industry. Other competitors have certainly emerged to challenge IBM's dominance, such as Dell, Compaq, and Hewlett-Packard, but in the volatile tech market of recent years, Big Blue was one of the steadiest of all computer technology stocks. The company is still a world leader in several areas of the computer technology market. It has about 320,000 employees and a market capitalization of about $200 billion.

Mercury Computer Systems
199 Riverneck Road
Chelmsford, MA 01824
978-256-1300
Nasdaq: MRCY
www.mc.com

Superman was known to use his X-ray vision to see through walls and behind closed doors. Mercury Computer Systems has honed its own see-through technology to help doctors see inside the human body and help military commanders see behind enemy lines. The firm manufactures digital signal processing computer systems that transform sensor generated data into information that can be displayed as images for human interpretation or subjected to additional computer analysis. The company has about 500 employees and a market capitalization of about $1 billion.

Network Appliance, Inc.
495 East Java Drive
Sunnyvale, CA 94089
408-822-6000

Nasdaq: NTAP
www.networkappliance.com

As companies expand their computer networks, they also must add more storage disks to keep up with the increasing flow of information. But with added disks comes added complexity in locating information on that network. Network Appliance helps solve that problem by making a computer storage device called a "filer" that companies can use to store and retrieve data on their networks quickly and efficiently. Network Appliance has about 1,500 employees and a market capitalization of about $7 billion.

Sun Microsystems, Inc.
901 San Antonio Road
Palo Alto, CA 94303
650-960-1300
Nasdaq: SUNW
www.sun.com

One of the brightest lights in the high-tech galaxy is Sun Microsystems, a maker of sophisticated workstations, storage devices, and servers. Sun has about 38,000 employees and a market capitalization of about $70 billion.

COMPUTER TECHNOLOGY

Semiconductors

Advanced Micro Devices
One AMD Place
Sunnyvale, CA 94088
408-732-2400
NYSE: AMD
www.amd.com

Advanced Micro Devices (AMD) created the world's fastest, most-powerful microprocessor for the PC in the form of its Athlon chip in the ever-escalating battle with Intel for supremacy in the semiconductor market. AMD holds a solid second place position in the lucrative microprocessor industry behind Intel. Founded in 1969, AMD has about 14,000 employees and a market capitalization of about $6 billion.

Altera Corporation
101 Innovation Drive
San Jose, CA 95134
408-544-7000
Nasdaq: ALTR
www.altera.com

Altera specializes in the production of microchips that can be programmed by engineers quickly and easily with software that runs on personal computers or engineering workstations. Altera's leading product is the programmable logic chip, which is used to set up many of the standard functions in computers, telephones, data communications equipment, and industrial applications. Founded in 1983, Altera has about 2,000 employees and a market capitalization of about $9 billion.

Analog Devices, Inc.
One Technology Way
Norwood, MA 02062
781-329-4700
NYSE: ADI
www.analogdevices.com

Founded in 1965, Analog Devices continues to find new and better ways to monitor and measure real-world phenomena such as temperature, pressure, sound, speed, and acceleration. The company makes about 2,000 products, most of which use high-performance integrated circuits that incorporate analog mixed signal and digital signal processing technologies. The company has about 9,000 employees and a market capitalization of about $13 billion.

Applied Materials

3050 Bowers Avenue
Santa Clara, CA 95054
408-727-5555
Nasdaq: AMAT
www.appliedmaterials.com

The world has developed an insatiable appetite for microchips. And Applied Materials, the world's largest manufacturer of semiconductor manufacturing equipment, is only too happy to meet the demand. Founded in 1967, the company has about 19,000 employees and a market capitalization of about $38 billion.

Broadcom Corporation

16215 Alton Parkway
Irvine, CA 92618
949-450-8700
Nasdaq: BRCM
www.broadcom.com

Broadcom's high bandwidth microchips have helped bring "convergence" to the Internet. The company's innovative microchips are designed to enable high-speed communications devices to merge voice, video, and data into a single common Internet medium. Broadcom has about 1,100 employees and a market capitalization of about $8 billion.

Intel Corporation

2200 Mission College Boulevard
Santa Clara, CA 95052
408-765-8080
Nasdaq: INTC
www.intel.com

Intel is the world's leading manufacturer of microchips. Its line of Pentium chips has been installed in millions of computers, serving as the control center of the personal computer by processing system data and controlling other devices in the system. Founded in 1968, the Santa Clara, California company has been the world leader in the microchip market since the mid-1980s, after designing the original microprocessor for the IBM PC. Intel has about 70,000 employees and a market capitalization of $200 billion.

Linear Technology Corporation

1630 McCarthy Boulevard
Milpitas, CA 95035
408-432-1900
Nasdaq: LLTC
www.linear-tech.com

Linear Technology makes microchips that are used in a wide range of applications, including wireless communications, notebook and hand-held computers, computer peripherals, medical systems, factory automation, network products, satellites, military and space systems, and automotive electronics. Founded in 1981, the company has about 2,800 employees and a market capitalization of about $14 billion.

Maxim Integrated Products

120 San Gabriel Drive
Sunnyvale, CA 94086

408-737-7600
Nasdaq: MXIM
www.maxim-ic.com

Maxim Integrated Products makes semiconductors used in a wide variety of applications, from cell phones to bar-code readers. In all, the company markets more than 2,000 products, many of which are used on microprocessor-based electronics equipment, such as personal computers and peripherals, test equipment, handheld devices, wireless phones and pagers, and video displays. Founded in 1983, Maxim has about 4,200 employees and 1,000 shareholders and has a market capitalization of about $15 billion.

Microchip Technology, Inc.
2355 West Chandler Boulevard
Chandler, AZ 85224
480-792-7200
Nasdaq: MCHP
www.microchip.com

Tiny microcontrollers serve as the brains of thousands of modern devices, from TV remote controls and garage door openers to handheld tools, cell phones, and major appliances. Microchip Technology is one of the leading makers of microcontrollers and related products. First incorporated in 1989, Microchip Technology has about 2,700 employees and a market capitalization of about $4 billion.

Novellus Systems, Inc.
4000 North First Street
San Jose, CA 95134
408-943-9700
Nasdaq: NVLS
www.novellus.com

Novellus is a leading maker of semiconductor manufacturing equipment. Founded in 1984, Novellus has continued to find new ways to manufacture smaller, more powerful chips. It has about 3,000 employees and a market capitalization of about $7 billion.

NVIDIA Corporation
3535 Monroe Street
Santa Clara, CA 95051
408-615-2500
Nasdaq: NVDA
www.nvidia.com

NVIDIA puts the 3D in computer graphics. The Santa Clara, California, operation is the worldwide leader in graphics processors and media communications devices. NVIDIA offers a full range of semiconductor-based graphics processors for 3D, 2D, video, audio, communications, and high-definition digital video and television. Its products work on workstations, mobile PCs, and Internet-enabled appliances. It has about 800 employees and a market capitalization of about $6 billion.

PMC-Sierra, Inc.
900 East Hamilton Avenue, Suite 250
Campbell, CA 95008
408-626-2000
Nasdaq: PMCS
www.pmcsierra.com

PMC-Sierra helps its manufacturing customers conform to network standards by designing semiconductor-based products that perform the most common networking functions and can be used in the majority of applications used in the Internet infrastructure. The company designs products for a wide variety of networking equipment. It has about 1,700 employees and a market capitalization of about $7 billion.

Semtech Corporation
652 Mitchell Road
Newbury Park, CA 91320
805-498-2111
Nasdaq: SMTC
www.semtech.com

Semtech manufactures semiconductors used to control and protect computers and other electronic devices. At one time, the company's products were used almost exclusively for military applications. Over the past six years, Semtech has expanded its customer base dramatically, with corporate clients in the communications, computer, video, test equipment, and commercial electronics markets. Semtech has about 800 employees and a market capitalization of about $2 billion.

Xilinx, Inc.
2100 Logic Drive
San Jose, CA 95124
408-559-7778
Nasdaq: XLNX
www.xilinx.com

Faster time to market. That's the promise Xilinx microchips offer for electronics manufacturers. The company is the leading manufacturer of programmable logic chips, with a 42 percent share of the $4 billion market. Founded in 1984, Xilinx has been a pioneer in the development of programmable microchips and the software needed to program those chips. The company has about 2,000 employees and a market capitalization of about $15 billion.

COMPUTER TECHNOLOGY

Software

Adobe Systems, Inc.
345 Park Avenue
San Jose, CA 95110
408-536-6000
Nasdaq: ADBE
www.adobe.com

Stealing a page from Johann Gutenberg, Adobe launched a printing revolution of its own in 1984 by creating desktop publishing software. It has never looked back. Graphic designers, advertising creatives, newspaper and magazine publishers, and Web designers have used the company's leading-edge software to create, distribute, and manage information both online and on the printed page. Founded in 1982, the company has about 3,000 employees and a market capitalization of about $7 billion.

Avant! Corporation
46871 Bayside Parkway
Fremont, CA 94538
510-413-8000
Nasdaq: AVNT
www.avanticorp.com

As microchips get smaller and smaller, semiconductor design engineers require increasingly sophisticated tools to create the next generation of chips. Avant! Corporation makes specialized software that helps electronics engineers design advanced microscopic chips for such devices as cell phones, digital watches, and automotive components. It has about 1,000 employees and a market capitalization of about $327 million.

Citrix Systems, Inc.

6400 Northwest Sixth Way
Ft. Lauderdale, FL 33309
954-267-3000
Nasdaq: CTXS
www.citrix.com

Citrix Systems brings uniformity to the complex and divergent world of computer technology. The company's application server software gives companies the ability to run any application on any device over any connection from wireless to the Web. With Citrix software, companies can manage their applications without regard to location, network connection, or type of hardware platform. The company has about 1,400 employees and a market capitalization of about $5 billion.

Electronic Arts, Inc.

209 Redwood Shores Parkway
Redwood City, CA 94065
650-628-1500
Nasdaq: ERTS
www.ea.com

Every time Sony comes up with a new generation of its famous PlayStation or Nintendo upgrades its own video game software, they are creating a new profit opportunity for Electronic Arts. It is the world's leading independent video game manufacturer, pumping out a new crop of top-selling games year after year. Among its leading sellers are FIFA Soccer, Madden NFL (football), NASCAR, NBA Live (basketball), and PGA Tour Golf.

Microsoft Corporation
One Microsoft Way
Redmond, WA 98052
425-882-8080
Nasdaq: MSFT
www.microsoft.com

There will be no break-up of Microsoft, which no doubt instills fear in the hearts of its competitors. And with good reason. Founder Bill Gates has proven to be a ruthless and powerful foe in the software wars. Founded in 1975, Microsoft is the worldwide leader in software for personal computers. Microsoft has about 39,000 employees and a market capitalization of about $300 billion.

Oracle Corporation
500 Oracle Parkway
Redwood Shores, CA 94065
650-506-7000
Nasdaq: ORCL
www.oracle.com

Oracle is the world's second largest software maker behind Microsoft. The Redwood Shores, California operation specializes in database and development software, business applications for sales and service, manufacturing and supply chain applications, and finance and human resources software. Founded in 1977, Oracle has about 41,000 employees and a market capitalization of about $100 billion.

SunGard Data Systems, Inc.
1285 Drummers Lane, Suite 300
Wayne, PA 19087
610-341-8700
NYSE: SDS
www.sungard.com

SunGard Data Systems specializes in software and services that help banks and investment companies simplify the complex task of managing and investing their customers' money. The company has about 8,000 employees and a market capitalization of about $7 billion.

Veritas Software Corporation
350 Ellis Street
Mountain View, CA 94043
650-527-8000
Nasdaq: VRTS
www.veritas.com

There is no such thing as a fail-proof computer network protection system, but Veritas Software can make systems as secure as possible. Companies use Veritas software to ensure that their data is protected and accessible at all times. The firm has about 5,000 employees and a market capitalization of about $12 billion.

COMPUTER TECHNOLOGY

Internet Infrastructure

Check Point Software Technology
3A Jabotinsky Street
Ramat-Gan
52520 94065
Israel
650-628-2000
Nasdaq: CHKP
www.checkpoint.com

Internet security has been a continuing threat for PC owners and network systems operators alike. That threat has been money in the bank for Check Point Software, which is a world leader in developing Internet security software. Check Point founder and CEO Gil Schwed invented the firewall and is revered as one of the Internet's true pioneers. E-commerce wouldn't be possible without firewalls, which are security gateways that protect internal networks from hackers. The company has about 800 employees and a market capitalization of about $15 billion.

Cisco Systems

170 West Tasman Drive
San Jose, CA 95134
408-526-4100
Nasdaq: CSCO
www.cisco.com

Cisco Systems helps hold the World Wide Web together through its array of routers, switches, and access servers. The company supplies more than 80 percent of all routers used on the Internet backbone. Cisco also is the world's leading supplier of networking products for corporate intranets in addition to the global Internet. The company has about 30,000 employees and a market capitalization of about $130 billion.

Internet Security Systems

6303 Barfield Road
Atlanta, GA 30328
404-236-2943
Nasdaq: ISSX
www.isscorp.com

Hackers and computer viruses remain a constant threat to corporate and government computer networks around the world. Internet Security Systems (ISS) designs and manufactures network security monitoring, detection, and response software that protects the security and integrity of computer databases and networks. The ISS system not only repels hackers, but also it detects and monitors each attempt. It has about 1,200 employees and a market capitalization of about $1 billion.

Juniper Networks, Inc.

1194 North Mathilda Avenue
Sunnyvale, CA 94089
408-745-2000
Nasdaq: JNPR
www.juniper.net

Telecommunications companies looking for the best and fastest routers on the market once turned exclusively to Cisco Systems. Now Juniper Networks is capturing a growing share of the market, because its high-speed routers—which are used to transmit data across the Internet—are the fastest in the business. The company has about 350 employees and a market capitalization of about $12 billion.

Mercury Interactive Corporation

1325 Borregas Avenue
Sunnyvale, CA 94089
408-822-5200
Nasdaq: MERQ
www.mercuryinteractive.com

There seems to be no end to the number of problems an Internet company can encounter trying to keep its site up and running. Mercury Interactive makes software that enables Internet companies to test their Web functions and isolate bad links, slow applications, and a host of other potential problems. Mercury Interactive has about 850 employees and a market capitalization of about $3 billion.

VeriSign, Inc.

1350 Charleston Road
Mountain View, CA 94043
650-961-7500
Nasdaq: VRSN
www.verisign.com

VeriSign helps businesses get up and running on the World Wide Web. The company offers domain name registration, digital security certificates, and global registry and payment services that provide the critical Web identity, authentication, and transaction infrastructure online businesses need to establish a Web presence. The company has about 2,300 employees and a market capitalization of about $11 billion.

Verity, Inc.
894 Ross Drive
Sunnyvale, CA 94089
408-541-1500
Nasdaq: VRTY
www.verity.com

Verity's industry-leading search engine software picks up where other Internet search engines leave off, ferreting out very specific information instantly on an unlimited range of topics. The company's software serves the role of an online librarian by quickly searching, filtering, displaying, and saving information stored on corporate databases, intranets, CD-ROMs, and the Internet, using classification standards developed by librarians. The company has about 370 employees and a market capitalization of about $1 billion.

COMPUTER TECHNOLOGY

E-commerce

Amazon.com, Inc.
1200 12th Avenue South, Suite 1200
Seattle, WA 98144
206-266-1000
Nasdaq: AMZN
www.amazon.com

Launched in 1995 as an online retailer of books, Amazon has steadily added new products to the mix. It is the leading Internet seller of books, music, and videos. In all, it lists about 28 million unique items at its site, including toys, electronics, cameras, software, games, hardware, lawn and patio items, and wireless products. Amazon claims about 30 million customers worldwide. Amazon.com went public with its initial stock offering in 1997. It has about 7,000 employees and a market capitalization of about $4 billion.

AOL Time Warner, Inc.

75 Rockefeller Plaza
New York, NY 10019
212-484-8000
NYSE: AOL
www.timewarner.com

Never before has a single company dominated so many media channels. With its acquisition of Time Warner, America Online became the world's leading media conglomerate. In addition to its own online presence, AOL Time Warner now commands a diversified array of magazines, television stations, and other media assets. AOL is the world's leading Internet portal with more than 30 million subscribers.

DoubleClick, Inc.

450 West 33rd Street
New York, NY 10001
212-683-0001
Nasdaq: DCLK
www.doubleclick.com

Like many of the nation's elite advertising agencies, DoubleClick has its headquarters on New York's Madison Avenue. But there is something very different about DoubleClick. The company focuses exclusively on online advertising. DoubleClick is the leader of the online advertising market, helping Web publishers large and small attract advertisers to their sites. DoubleClick has about 2,000 employees and a market capitalization of about $2 billion.

eBay, Inc.
2145 Hamilton Avenue
San Jose, CA 95125
408-558-7400
Nasdaq: EBAY
www.ebay.com

In the great e-commerce meltdown, more than 2,000 e-tailers gave up the ghost, and scores of others were left gasping for air. But eBay held tough, standing alone as the one online economic business model that actually works. Founded in 1995, eBay is the flea market to the world. As the world's biggest online auction, eBay moves one of humanity's most primordial urges—bargain hunting—off the fairgrounds parking lot and onto the Web. It has about 140 employees and a market capitalization of about $10 billion.

Yahoo! Inc.
3420 Central Expressway
Santa Clara, CA 95051
408-731-3300
Nasdaq: YHOO
www.yahoo.com

Yahoo! may well be the world's most popular spot. Nearly 200 million Web surfers use the Internet portal service each month for news, online shopping, and search engine services. On average, Yahoo! logs nearly one billion page views per day! Yahoo! is the leading Internet portal in terms of traffic, advertising, and household and business user reach. It has about 3,000 employees and a market capitalization of about $11 billion.

CONSTRUCTION

Toll Brothers, Inc.
3103 Philmont Avenue
Huntingdon Valley, PA 19006
215-938-8000
NYSE: TOL
www.tollbrothers.com

Toll Brothers is in the business of building the American dream—and it does it by the thousands. In all, the company has built more than 15,000 homes in 321 communities, and the numbers continue to grow. Toll now builds about 4,000 new homes a year. The company has about 2,500 employees and a market capitalization of about $1.5 billion.

CONSUMER PRODUCTS

Colgate-Palmolive Company
300 Park Avenue
New York, NY 10022
212-310-2000
NYSE: CL
www.colgatepalmolive.com

Colgate-Palmolive helps fend off cavities the world over. The New York operation accounts for about half of all toothpaste sold worldwide. It markets its toothpaste and other products in more than 200 countries. Foreign sales account for about 70 percent of the company's $9 billion in annual revenue. Colgate-Palmolive has about 38,000 employees, 45,000 shareholders, and a market capitalization of about $34 billion.

Jones Apparel Group, Inc.

250 Rittenhouse Circle
Bristol, PA 19007
215-785-4000
NYSE: JNY
www.jonesapparel.com

Jones Apparel not only makes a full line of women's clothing, it also operates about 1,000 stores to sell its goods. The company makes a long line of popular brands of shoes, accessories, and apparel. Jones has about 19,000 employees and a market capitalization of about $5 billion.

The Procter & Gamble Company

One Procter & Gamble Plaza
Cincinnati, OH 45202
513-983-1100
NYSE: PG
www.pg.com

If you're like millions of Americans, Procter & Gamble has invaded nearly every closet and cupboard of your house. From dish soaps and laundry detergents to coffee and cosmetics, the Cincinnati operation puts more than 300 product brands on the market, including Tide, Cheer, Ivory, Bounce, and a host of other familiar names. P&G has 110,000 employees, about 275,000 shareholders, and a market capitalization of about $80 billion.

ELECTRONICS AND ELECTRICAL PRODUCTS

Emerson Electric Company

8000 West Florissant Avenue
P.O. Box 4100
St. Louis, MO 63136
314-533-2000

NYSE: EMR

www.emersonelectric.com

After 43 consecutive years of record earnings, Emerson Electric Company's streak finally ended in fiscal 2001. But sales revenue continues to climb, and the company is still making solid profits on its vast line of electrical and electronic products and systems for the industrial and commercial markets. The 111-year-old operation manufactures a wide range of motors for industrial and heavy commercial applications, industrial automation equipment, gear drives, power distribution equipment, and temperature and environmental control systems.

General Electric Company

3135 Easton Turnpike

Fairfield, CT 06431

203-373-2211

NYSE: GE

www.ge.com

This is the house that Jack built—long after Thomas A. Edison laid the foundation. Jack Welch, who retired in late 2001 as chairman and CEO of General Electric, spent his two decades at the helm of GE turning it into the nation's largest capitalization company. The company has posted record earnings for 25 consecutive years. Part of GE's growth has been through acquisitions, acquiring more than 100 companies a year for the past five years. GE has about 290,000 employees and 530,000 shareholders and has a market capitalization of about $450 billion.

Molex, Inc.

2222 Wellington Court

Lisle, IL 60532

630-969-4550

Nasdaq: MOLX

www.molex.com

Molex manufactures more than 100,000 electronic, electrical, and fiber-optic interconnection products and switches. It is the second largest connector manufacturer in the world. Molex has about 18,000 employees and 12,000 shareholders and has a market capitalization of about $7 billion.

ENERGY

AstroPower, Inc.
Solar Park
Newark, NJ 19716
302-366-0400
Nasdaq: APWR
www.astropower.com

Rising oil prices continue to fuel the growth of AstroPower, which is a leading manufacturer of solar electric power products. The Delaware-based operation makes solar cells, modules, and panels. AstroPower's solar sells are semiconductor devices that convert sunlight into electricity and form the building block for all solar electric power products. Founded in 1983, AstroPower has about 350 employees and a market capitalization of about $500 million.

ChevronTexaco Corporation
575 Market Street
San Francisco, CA 94105
415-894-7700
NYSE: CVX
www.chevron.com

ChevronTexaco is best known for its petroleum operations, including about 8,000 service stations in the United States. But with operations in about 100 countries, Chevron also has its hands in other areas of the energy industry, including coal mining and chemical production. The company reached a merger agreement with Texaco in late 2001. The combined company, ChevronTexaco, is the third largest oil and gas producer in the United States.

FOOD AND BEVERAGES

Anheuser-Busch Companies, Inc.
One Busch Place
St. Louis, MO 63118
314-577-2000
NYSE: BUD
www.anheuser-busch.com

The suds keep flowing and the profits keep growing for Anheuser-Busch, the world's leading brewery. Over the past quarter-century, the St. Louis operation has more than doubled its share of the domestic beer market, from about 23 percent in the late 1970s to about 50 percent in 2001. Worldwide it accounts for about 10 percent of all beer sales. The company has about 24,000 employees and 60,000 shareholders and has a market capitalization of about $36 billion.

Coca-Cola Company
One Coca-Cola Plaza
Atlanta, GA 30313
404-676-2121
NYSE: KO
www.cocacola.com

Coke may still be the "Real Thing," but it has 238 other siblings. In all, Coca-Cola puts out 239 different beverages, including soft drinks, sports drinks, juice, bottled water, teas, and coffees. The company also supplies 19 percent of all nonalcoholic, ready-to-drink beverages sold around the world. Founded in 1886, Coca-Cola has about 37,000 employees and 366,000 shareholders and has a market capitalization of about $110 billion.

ConAgra Foods, Inc.
One ConAgra Drive
Omaha, NE 68102
402-595-4707
NYSE: CAG
www.conagra.com

From feeds and fertilizer to Banquet chickens and Peter Pan peanut butter, ConAgra covers nearly every furrow and fowl of the agricultural industry. But ConAgra's bread and butter is its grocery and refrigerated foods divisions. It is the second largest food supplier in the world, with annual sales of about $27 billion. ConAgra has about 85,000 employees, 165,000 shareholders, and a market capitalization of about $12 billion.

Hershey Foods Company
100 Crystal A Drive
Hershey, PA 17033
717-534-6799
NYSE: HSY
www.hersheys.com

In this country, Hershey has become almost synonymous with chocolate. But Hershey candies come in a lot more flavors than just chocolate. In all, the company offers more than 50 brands of candies. It is the nation's leading confectionery producer, with about a 35 percent share of the $11 billion sweet tooth market. Founded in 1893, Hershey has about 14,000 employees, 44,000 shareholders, and a market capitalization of about $8 billion.

PepsiCo, Inc.

700 Anderson Hill Road
Purchase, NY 10577
914-253-2000
NYSE: PEP
www.pepsico.com

With its line of soft drinks, Frito-Lay chips, and Tropicana beverages, PepsiCo has been a willing co-conspirator in the fattening of America—while fattening its own balance sheet along the way. PepsiCo has about a 32 percent share of the U.S. soft drink market—ranking second to Coca-Cola—while its Frito-Lay division is far and away the market leader in snack chips both in the United States and around the world. The company has about 118,000 employees, 207,000 shareholders, and a market capitalization of about $65 billion.

Sara Lee Corporation

Three First National Plaza
Suite 4600
Chicago, IL 60602
312-726-2600
NYSE: SLE
www.saralee.com

Sara Lee made its name in frozen desserts, but it is making its fortune in bras and intimate apparel. This is no Victoria's Secret, but it *is* the world leader in the sale of women's intimate clothing and a leader in men's and boy's underwear and printed T-shirts. Among its leading brands are Hanes, Playtex, L'eggs, Isotoner, Sheer Energy, Wonderbra, and Champion. Sara Lee has about 155,000 employees, 85,000 shareholders, and a market capitalization of about $16 billion.

Sysco Corporation
1390 Enclave Parkway
Houston, TX 77077
281-584-1390
NYSE: SYK
www.sysco.com

Sysco delivers the meat and potatoes, the bread and butter, the milk and honey, the biscuits and gravy, and about 275,000 food products and related goods to food service operations around the country. It is the nation's largest marketer of food service products, with operations in the nation's 150 largest cities (plus parts of Canada). The company has about 40,000 employees, 15,000 shareholders, and a market capitalization of about $20 billion.

William Wrigley, Jr. & Company
410 North Michigan Avenue
Chicago, IL 60611
312-644-2121
NYSE: WWY
www.wrigley.com

Wrigley has turned chewing gum into a $2 billion business. From its humble beginnings 111 years ago, the Chicago chewing gum giant has spread its Juicy Fruit, Doublemint, Spearmint, and other brands to more than 140 countries around the world. It has about 9,800 employees, 37,000 shareholders, and a market capitalization of about $11 billion.

FOOD AND DRUG RETAIL

The Kroger Company
1014 Vine Street
Cincinnati, OH 45202

513-762-4000
NYSE: KR
www.kroger.com

Founded in 1883, Kroger has become the nation's largest grocery store chain, with more than 2,300 stores throughout the United States. The company builds three different types of grocery stores, including combination food and drug stores, multidepartment stores, and low-price warehouse stores. Kroger has about 315,000 full-time and part-time employees, 55,000 shareholders, and a market capitalization of about $20 billion.

Safeway, Inc.
5918 Stoneridge Mall Road
Pleasanton, CA 94588
925-467-3000
NYSE: SWY
www.safeway.com

The grocery business runs on thin margins and keen competition. Safeway has managed to keep profits growing by expanding its store base and its offerings. With 1,700 stores in about 20 states and 4 Canadian provinces, Safeway is one of North America's biggest grocery store chains. Safeway has about 190,000 employees and a market capitalization of about $28 billion.

Walgreen Company
200 Wilmot Road
Deerfield, IL 60015
847-940-2500
NYSE: WAG
www.walgreens.com

Charles Walgreen, Sr., opened the first Walgreen's pharmacy a century ago in 1901. Since then the Chicago-based retailer has become the nation's largest pharmacy chain, with more than 3,000 stores in 43 states and Puerto Rico. Walgreen serves about 3 million customers a day and dishes out about 300 million prescriptions per year—nearly 10 percent of all retail prescriptions filled in the United States. Walgreen has about 115,000 employees, 90,000 shareholders, and a market capitalization of about $40 billion.

INDUSTRIAL EQUIPMENT AND SUPPLIES

Danaher Corporation
2099 Pennsylvania Avenue, 12th Floor
Washington, DC 20006
202-828-0850
NYSE: DHR
www.danaher.com

The Danaher name may not be familiar to you, but if you know hand tools, you know Danaher. The company makes Craftsman tools, which has been a staple of Sears, Roebuck and Company for many years. Danaher is also a primary supplier of specialized automotive service tools and general purpose mechanics' hand tools for the 6,500 NAPA auto parts stores. Danaher has about 24,000 employees and a market capitalization of about $8 billion.

Dionex Corporation
1228 Titan Way
P.O. Box 3603
Sunnyvale, CA 94086
408-737-0700
Nasdaq: DNEX
www.dionex.com

As the requirements of advanced scientific research become increasingly complex, the sophistication of research equipment also must keep pace. Dionex makes a growing line of scientific research and analysis equipment, including instruments that can separate and quantify the individual components of complex chemical mixtures. Dionex has about 800 employees, 1,600 shareholders, and a market capitalization of about $700 million.

Donaldson Company, Inc.
1400 West 94th Street
Minneapolis, MN 55431
952-887-3131
NYSE: DCI
www.donaldson.com

Donaldson has declared war on dust, grime, and flying particles. The Minneapolis-based operation manufactures filters and purifiers for trucks, turbines, and a broad range of industrial and agricultural equipment. The company's biggest market is engine products, which account for about 61 percent of its total revenue. The company has about 8,500 employees and a market capitalization of about $1.5 billion.

Tyco International, Inc.
One Tyco Park
Exeter, NH 03833
603-778-9700
NYSE: TYC
www.tyco.com

Tyco International can help you get a better night's sleep—although bedding is not one of the many products Tyco manufactures. The company is a leading maker of fire detectors and security systems, so you'll sleep better once you're wired with Tyco. Tyco also operates divisions involved in a diverse mix of other areas, from pipes and plastics to electronics and medical supplies. Tyco has about 215,000 employees, 6,200 shareholders, and a market capitalization of about $93 billion.

United Technologies
United Technologies Building
One Financial Plaza
Hartford, CT 06101
860-728-7000
NYSE: UTX
www.utc.com

United Technologies is not what you'd call a new economy technology company. It doesn't make semiconductors or software. Its products are strictly *old school* technology—Carrier air conditioners, Otis elevators, Sikorsky helicopters, and Pratt & Whitney aircraft engines. Founded in 1934, United Technologies has about 150,000 employees and a market capitalization of about $35 billion.

INSURANCE AND HMOs

AFLAC, Inc.
1932 Wynnton Road
Columbus, GA 31999
706-323-3431
NYSE: AFL
www.aflac.com

AFLAC sells a line of supplemental insurance that is big in the United States and huge in Japan. In fact, one out of every five Japanese workers is insured by AFLAC, and its policies are offered to employees of 96 percent of the companies listed on the Tokyo Stock Exchange. AFLAC specializes in supplemental cancer coverage that helps fill the gaps in its customers' primary policies. It is the leading writer of cancer expense insurance worldwide. The company also sells life, accident, Medicare supplement, and long-term convalescent care policies. AFLAC has about 4,000 employees, 89,000 shareholders, and a market capitalization of about $15 billion.

American International Group, Inc.

70 Pine Street
New York, NY 10270
212-770-7000
NYSE: AIG
www.aig.com

American International Group (AIG) offers insurance coverage that covers the world. Not only is the New York–based operation the leading underwriter of commercial and industrial insurance in the United States, but it also provides insurance and financial services to customers in about 130 countries around the world. Worldwide, the company has about 40,000 employees and about 10,000 shareholders and has a market capitalization of about $190 billion.

Jefferson-Pilot Corporation

100 North Greene Street
Greensboro, NC 27401
336-691-3000
NYSE: JP
www.jpfinancial.com

Jefferson-Pilot can sell you life insurance, health insurance, and annuities—as well as some advertising spots on its group of radio and television stations. Although the company generates most of its revenue from its growing group of insurance products, it also has established a small presence in the broadcasting business. Jefferson-Pilot has about 3,800 employees and 10,000 stockholders and has a market capitalization of about $7 billion.

UnitedHealth Group, Inc.
UnitedHealth Group Center
9900 Bren Road East
Minnetonka, MN 55343
612-936-1300
NYSE: UNH
www.unitedhealthgroup.com

UnitedHealth Group is one of the nation's leading health maintenance organizations, with 35 million customers throughout the United States. Founded in 1974, the company has grown rapidly by aggressively acquiring smaller HMOs. The firm has about 30,000 employees, 4,600 shareholders, and a market capitalization of about $17 billion.

INVESTING AND FINANCIAL

Alliance Capital Management Holding LP
1345 Avenue of the Americas
New York, NY 10105
212-969-1000
NYSE: AC
www.alliancecapital.com

Alliance Capital Management is the nation's largest publicly traded asset management investment firm. Alliance manages about 120 mutual funds and provides investment management services to employee benefit plans for about a third of the Fortune 100 companies. The company, which is technically a limited partnership, has about 4,400 employees and 1,700 shareholders (technically they are considered "unit" holders). Alliance has a market capitalization of about $13 billion.

Franklin Resources, Inc.

777 Mariners Island Boulevard

San Mateo, CA 94404

650-312-2000

NYSE: BEN

www.franklintempleton.com

Franklin Resources rode the crest of the 1990s bull market to become one of the leading investment companies in the world. The firm manages more than $200 billion in mutual funds and other investments for individuals, institutions, and corporate pension plans. It has offices in 29 countries and clients in more than 130 countries. Founded in 1947, Franklin has about 4,000 shareholders, 6,300 employees, and a market capitalization of about $12 billion.

Legg Mason, Inc.

100 Light Street

Baltimore, MD 21202

410-539-0000

NYSE: LM

www.leggmason.com

Legg Mason is a financial services conglomerate that stretches like an octopus through much of the investment market. The Baltimore operation has a network of subsidiaries—some formed from within, others acquired—that cover the gamut of both the institutional and individual financial services markets. The company has about 5,400 employees, 2,300 shareholders, and a market capitalization of about $3 billion.

T. Rowe Price Group, Inc.

100 East Pratt Street

Baltimore, MD 21202

410-345-2000

Nasdaq: TROW

www.troweprice.com

No-load mutual funds with low annual expense ratios have been the stock in trade for T. Rowe Price. The Baltimore operation offers about 75 different stock, bond, and money market mutual funds. It also manages about 450 separate and commingled institutional accounts. In all, the company has about $160 billion of assets under management. T. Rowe Price has about 4,000 employees and a market capitalization of about $5 billion.

MEDICAL

Biotechnology

Affymetrix, Inc.
3380 Central Expressway
Santa Clara, CA 95051
408-731-5000
Nasdaq: AFFX
www.affymetrix.com

A pioneer on the genetic frontier, Affymetrix GeneChip technology provides researchers with the tools to quickly and accurately process genetic data as they explore the recently mapped human genome. Affymetrix technology allows researchers to identify, analyze, and manage complex genetic information. Founded in 1992, the company has about 500 employees and a market capitalization of about $3 billion.

Amgen, Inc.
One Amgen Center Drive
Thousand Oakes, CA 91320
805-447-1000
Nasdaq: AMGN
www.Amgen.com

Long before stem cells and human cloning were part of the American vernacular, Amgen was quietly researching and developing the new frontiers of medical technology. Founded in 1980, Amgen is one of the true pioneers of the biotechnology revolution. The Silicon Valley operation is the world's largest independent biotechnology company. Amgen has about 7,300 employees and a market capitalization of about $67 billion.

Applied Biosystems Group

761 Main Avenue
Norwalk, CT 06859
203-762-1000
NYSE: ABI
www.appliedbiosystems.com

In the complex world of biotechnology, Applied Biosystems makes the tools that scientists need to solve the mysteries of DNA. The Norwalk, Connecticut operation develops instrument-based systems, reagents, and software for biotechnology research. Founded in 1981, the company has about 4,000 employees and a market capitalization of about $10 billion.

Biogen, Inc.

14 Cambridge Center
Cambridge, MA 02142
617-679-2000
Nasdaq: BGEN
www.biogen.com

A single product accounts for the vast majority of Biogen's $926 million in total revenue, but the Cambridge, Massachusetts operation is trying hard to develop its next winner. The company currently has 20 research products under way in the areas of immunology, cancer, neuroscience, and fibrosis. Founded in 1978, Biogen is one of the nation's oldest biotech companies. Its leading product is Avonex, which is the world's leading multiple sclerosis treatment. Biogen has about 1,500 employees and a market capitalization of about $9 billion.

Genentech, Inc.
One DNA Way
South San Francisco, CA 94080
650-225-1000
NYSE: DNA
www.gene.com

Genentech put the "DNA" in modern medicine. The 25-year-old operation has been a pioneer in the development of biotech medications. The San Francisco operation (whose stock symbol is DNA) currently has nine approved medications on the market that are used to address a broad range of serious medical conditions, and it has another 20 active projects in the pipeline. Genentech has about 4,500 employees and a market capitalization of about $27 billion.

MedImmune, Inc.
35 West Watkins Mill Road
Gaithersburg, MD 20878
301-417-0770
Nasdaq: MEDI
www.medimmune.com

MedImmune helps children—and their parents—breathe easier. The company's flagship product, Synagis, is designed to combat respiratory synctial virus (RSV), which is the leading cause of lower respiratory illness in children. Synagis produces about 90 percent of the company's sales. Founded in 1987, the company has about 800 employees and a market capitalization of about $9 billion.

MEDICAL

Pharmaceuticals and Medical Products

Abbott Laboratories
100 Abbott Park Road
Abbott Park, IL 60064-6400
847-937-6100
NYSE: ABT
www.abbott.com

For well over a century, Abbott Laboratories has been developing drugs and diagnostic testing products for doctors and hospitals the world over. Founded in 1888, the Chicago operation is one of the world's leading makers of blood screening equipment and was the first company to introduce an AIDS antibody test. With 30 consecutive years of increased sales and earnings, Abbott has grown to about 60,000 employees and 107,000 shareholders. It has a market capitalization of about $75 billion.

Biomet, Inc.
56 East Bell Drive
Warsaw, IN 46582
219-267-6639
Nasdaq: BMET
www.biomet.com

Hip on the blink, knee gone numb, shoulder in shambles? Biomet has the fix for what ails you. The company specializes in reconstructive devices used to replace joints that have degenerated due to arthritis, osteoporosis, or injury. Incorporated in 1977, Biomet has about 4,000 employees and 7,000 shareholders. It has a market capitalization of about $8 billion.

Bristol-Myers Squibb Company

345 Park Avenue
New York, NY 10154
212-546-4000
NYSE: BMY
www.bristolmyers.com

Bristol-Myers Squibb puts out a long list of products designed to combat cancer, squelch headaches, and heal heart conditions. Its line of over-the-counter medications, such as Excedrin, Nuprin, and Bufferin, are permanent fixtures in millions of medicine cabinets across America. Founded in 1887, Bristol-Myers merged with Squibb in 1989. The company has about 55,000 employees and 135,000 shareholders and has a market capitalization of about $110 billion.

Cardinal Health

7000 Cardinal Place
Dublin, OH 43017
614-757-5000
NYSE: CAH
www.cardinal.com

Cardinal Health serves as a lifeline between medical manufacturers and the health care industry. The Dublin, Ohio operation has used an aggressive series of acquisitions to become one of the nation's leading distributors of pharmaceuticals and related health care products to drugstores, hospitals, care centers, and pharmacy departments of supermarkets and mass merchandisers. Cardinal has about 42,000 employees and a market capitalization of about $32 billion.

Johnson & Johnson

One Johnson & Johnson Plaza
New Brunswick, NJ 08933
732-524-0400

NYSE: JNJ

www.jnj.com

Johnson & Johnson is renowned worldwide for its line of baby care powders, oils, and related products. It also produces a number of other products that have become household names here and around the world, such as Band-Aids, Tylenol, Imodium A-D, and Mylanta antacid. Founded in 1887, Johnson & Johnson has about 100,000 employees, 170,000 shareholders, and a market capitalization of about $135 billion.

Eli Lilly & Company

Lilly Corporate Center

Indianapolis, IN 46285

317-276-2000

NYSE: LLY

www.elililly.com

Eli Lilly is well known for its breakthrough pharmaceuticals, such as Prozac and Ceclor, but the company's major focus is to become the pharmaceutical industry's "partner of choice." The Indianapolis operation is currently involved in more than 140 research and development collaborations with other companies and universities. Lilly has about 36,000 employees, 59,000 shareholders, and a market capitalization of about $86 billion.

Medtronic, Inc.

710 Medtronic Parkway N.E.

Minneapolis, MN 55422

763-514-4000

NYSE: MDT

www.medtronic.com

When Vice President Dick Cheney needed to shore up his ailing heart, surgeons installed a special pacemaker made by Medtronic. The company is the world's leading manufacturer of heart pacemakers and other implantable biomedical devices. It markets its products in more than 120 countries. Founded in 1949 and incorporated in 1957, Medtronic has about 25,000 employees, 42,500 shareholders, and a market capitalization of about $55 billion.

Merck & Company, Inc.
P.O. Box 100
One Merck Drive
Whitehouse Station, NJ 08889
908-423-1000
NYSE: MRK
www.merck.com

As many of Merck's leading pharmaceutical products head for the generic ranks, the company is betting its future on a handful of new and recently released medications to keep its bottom line growing. Founded in 1881, Merck is the world's leading maker of pharmaceuticals. The company has about 70,000 employees, 270,000 shareholders, and a market capitalization of about $154 billion.

Pfizer, Inc.
235 East 42nd Street
New York, NY 10017
212-573-2323
NYSE: PFE
www.pfizer.com

With 5 of the world's top 20 selling medicines, Pfizer has become one of the true leaders of the pharmaceutical industry. The company has eight different medicines that generate more than $1 billion a year in revenue. Perhaps best known of all of the company's offerings is Viagra, the world's leading impotence remedy. The company has about

75,000 employees, 147,000 shareholders, and a market capitalization of about $260 billion.

Schering-Plough Corporation
2000 Galloping Hill Road
Kenilworth, NJ 07033
908-298-4000
NYSE: SGP
www.schering-plough.com

In a single dose, Claritin can fight off allergies and relieve running noses for a full 24 hours. The wonder drug also does wonders for Schering-Plough's bottom line. Claritin is the world's best-selling antihistamine. With sales of just over $3 billion, it accounts for nearly a third of Schering-Plough's $10 billion in total annual revenue. The company has about 28,000 employees, 49,000 shareholders, and a market capitalization of about $56 billion.

Stryker Corporation
P.O. Box 4085
Kalamazoo, MI 49003
616-385-2600
NYSE: SYK
www.strykercorp.com

Known for its surgical instruments, artificial limbs, and other orthopedic products, Stryker is becoming increasingly diversified in its medical offerings. With 23 consecutive years of increased earnings and revenue, the firm continues to keep its customers at the leading edge of medical technology. The company has about 12,000 employees, 3,000 stockholders, and a market capitalization of $11 billion.

MEDICAL

Health Care Services

Universal Health Services, Inc.
Universal Corporate Center
367 South Gulph Road
King of Prussia, PA 19406
610-768-3300
NYSE: UHS
www.uhsinc.com

Care of the sick and injured is a growth industry in the United States, where the population is expanding and aging. Universal Health Services has been capitalizing on that trend by putting together a national chain of hospitals and health care centers. It is the nation's third largest investor-owned hospital chain, with a total of about 100 facilities. The company has about 26,000 employees and a market capitalization of about $2.5 billion.

OFFICE EQUIPMENT AND SUPPLIES

Avery Dennison Corporation
Miller Corporate Center
150 North Orange Grove Boulevard
Pasadena, CA 91103
626-304-2000
NYSE: AVY
www.averydennison.com

Avery Dennison is one of the world's leading manufacturers of self-adhesive materials, labels, tapes, and specialty chemical adhesives. The Pasadena, California operation has 200 manufacturing plants and sales offices in 42 countries around the world. Founded in 1946, the company has about 18,000 employees and a market capitalization of about $6 billion.

Pitney Bowes, Inc.
1 Elmcroft Road
Stamford, CT 06926
203-356-5000
NYSE: PBI
www.pitneybowes.com

For a company that relies on mailing services for most of its income, the advent of e-mail could have been a critical blow. But Pitney Bowes has continued to build its business by embracing new technologies rather than running from them, including a service offering postage to client companies instantly over the Internet. Pitney is the world's largest maker of postage meters and mailing equipment. It has about 29,000 employees and a market capitalization of about $10 billion.

PACKAGING

Bemis Company
222 South Ninth Street, Suite 2300
Minneapolis, MN 55402-4099
612-376-3003
NYSE: BMS
www.bemis.com

Whether they wrap it, sack it, box it, or bag it, Bemis makes the packaging for hundreds of foods, candies, medical products, and household goods. The 143-year-old Minneapolis operation is North America's largest manufacturer of flexible packaging. Bemis has about 11,000 employees and 6,000 shareholders and has a market capitalization of about $2 billion.

RESTAURANTS

McDonald's Corporation

McDonald's Plaza
Oak Brook, IL 60523
630-623-3000
NYSE: MCD
www.mcdonalds.com

No matter where you go in the world, it's hard to escape the shadow of the golden arches. Even American Samoa and French Guiana opened new McDonald's restaurants recently, bringing to 120 the total number of countries around the world that offer McDonald's fare. In all, about half of the company's 30,000 restaurants are located outside the United States. Foreign operations account for about 45 percent of total sales and 52 percent of operating profit. McDonald's has about 413,000 employees, 954,000 shareholders, and a market capitalization of about $40 billion.

Sonic Corporation

101 Park Avenue
Oklahoma City, OK 73102
405-280-7654
Nasdaq: SONC
www.sonicdrivein.com

There's a Sonic boom across the entire southern half of the United States. More than 2,000 Sonic restaurants have popped up across the warmer stretches of America, from California to southern Florida. The Oklahoma City fast-food operation is the largest drive-in restaurant chain in the nation. Founded in 1953, Sonic has about 250 corporate employees and a market capitalization of about $700 million.

Starbucks Corporation

2401 Utah Avenue South
P.O. Box 34067
Seattle, WA 98134
206-318-1575
Nasdaq: SBUX
www.starbucks.com

Starbucks has turned the coffee house experience into a $2 billion operation. Coffee drinkers can now get their morning caffeine buzz at more than 4,500 Starbucks restaurants across America and around the world. Founded in 1971, Starbucks has about 47,000 employees, 9,000 shareholders, and a market capitalization of about $7 billion.

RETAIL

Bed Bath & Beyond, Inc.

650 Liberty Avenue
Union, NJ 07083
908-688-0888
Nasdaq: BBBY
www.bedbathandbeyond.com

The warehouse superstore has moved into the bedroom with Bed Bath and Beyond (BBB). But this is no sleeper. The New Jersey retailer continues to rack up record earnings and revenue year after year. Bed Bath & Beyond stores offer a massive selection of home furnishings, bedroom and bathroom furniture and accessories, kitchen textiles, cookware, dinnerware, and other basic housewares. Bed Bath and Beyond has about 12,000 employees and a market capitalization of about $7 billion.

Best Buy Company, Inc.
7075 Flying Cloud Drive
Eden Prairie, MN 55344
952-947-2000
NYSE: BBY
www.bestbuy.com

For electronics junkies, Best Buy is the closest thing to heaven. The nation's largest retailer of consumer electronics, personal computers, entertainment software, and appliances operates more than 400 stores throughout the United States. The company has about 45,000 employees, 1,700 shareholders, and a market capitalization of about $11 billion.

Home Depot, Inc.
2455 Paces Ferry Road N.W.
Atlanta, GA 30339
770-433-8211
NYSE: HD
www.homedepot.com

Americans' love affair with home improvement has helped turn Home Depot into one of the most successful retailers in the world. The Atlanta-based operation has about 1,150 home improvement stores throughout North America. The company has about 227,000 employees, 61,000 shareholders, and a market capitalization of about $110 billion.

Kohl's Corporation
N56 W17000 Ridgewood Drive
Menomonee Falls, WI 53051
262-703-7000
NYSE: KSS
www.kohls.com

Name brand merchandise at modest prices has helped Kohl's become one of the nation's fastest growing retailers. The department store chain has grown from 40 stores in 1986 to more than 350 stores in 28 states today. It has about 17,000 full-time employees and 27,000 part-time employees, 6,000 shareholders, and a market capitalization of about $19 billion.

Wal-Mart Stores, Inc.
702 Southwest 8th Street
Bentonville, AR 72716
501-273-4000
NYSE: WMT
www.walmartstores.com

First America, then the world. Wal-Mart has taken its low prices to markets the world over. In recent years, the company has opened more than 1,000 stores in Europe, Asia, and Latin America. Wal-Mart is the world's largest retail chain, with more than 4,000 stores in all. The company operates about 1,750 discount stores in the United States, plus 900 Supercenters and 500 Sam's Clubs. Wal-Mart has about 1,250,000 employees, 300,000 shareholders, and a market capitalization of about $230 billion.

TELECOMMUNICATIONS

Nokia Corporation
Keilalahdentie 4, PL 226
FIN-00045
Espoo, Finland
905-427-6654
NYSE: NOK
www.nokia.com

The world has gone wireless with Nokia leading the way. Nokia is the world's leading manufacturer of mobile phones and a leading supplier of mobile Internet and broadband systems. The Finland-based operation is global in scope, with manufacturing plants in 10 countries and sales operations in 130 countries. Nokia has about 60,000 employees and a market capitalization of about $150 billion.

Polycom, Inc.
1565 Barber Lane
Milpitas, CA 95035
408-474-2000
Nasdaq: PLCM
www.polycom.com

Polycom's ViaVideo can turn your home computer into a video telephone, and its ViewStation units can turn any room in your business into a videoconference center. Polycom is the world market leader in video and voiceconferencing products. The company offers a full line of voice and video communications equipment for businesses and individuals. Founded in 1990, Polycom has about 550 employees and a market capitalization of about $2 billion.

Verizon Communications
1095 Avenue of the Americas, 36th Floor
New York, NY 10036
212-395-2121
NYSE: VZ
www.verizon.com

What's on the horizon for Verizon? A larger presence in the fast-growing fields of data communication and wireless communications is a top priority for the telecommunications giant that was created by the 2000 merger of GTE and Bell Atlantic. The company has about 260,000 employees and a market capitalization of about $132 billion.

ViaSat, Inc.
6155 El Camino Real
Carlsbad, CA 92009
760-476-2200
Nasdaq: VSAT
www.viasat.com

Once the play toys of NASA, satellites have become an important part of the communications network. ViaSat is a leading manufacturer of digital satellite telecommunications and wireless signal processing equipment. The firm utilizes Demand Assigned Multiple Access (DAMA) technology, which allows large numbers of satellite subscribers to share common satellite transponders for high-performance voice, fax, or data communications. The company has about 350 employees and a market capitalization of about $400 million.

Vodafone Group PLC
The Courtyard, 2-4
London Road
Newbury, Berkshire
RG14 1JX, United Kingdom
800-233-5601
NYSE: VOD
www.vodafone.com

Vodafone wants to create a seamless worldwide mobile phone network. The world's largest wireless company is well on its way to that goal with ownership stakes in wireless carriers in some 30 countries throughout Asia/Pacific, Europe, the United States, Africa, and the Middle East. Vodafone has about 29,000 employees and a market capitalization of about $160 billion.

TRANSPORTATION

Harley-Davidson, Inc.

3700 West Juneau Avenue
Milwaukee, WI 53208
414-342-4680
NYSE: HDI
www.harley-davidson.com

The hogs keep rolling and Harley-Davidson keeps growing. The Milwaukee-based operation continues to be the hottest thing on wheels, with 15 consecutive years of record earnings and revenue. Although consumers have faced long delays on some Harley models—and many Asian and European consumers are simply unable to get their hands on a Harley no matter how long the wait—Harley has refused to accelerate its manufacturing process simply to meet demand. It has opened some new plants, but management will not compromise the quality of its bikes to crank up the quantity. Founded in 1903, Harley-Davidson has about 7,500 employees and 35,000 shareholders and has a market capitalization of about $15 billion.

Southwest Airlines Company

P.O. Box 36611
Dallas, TX 75235
214-792-4000
NYSE: LUV
www.southwest.com

It's been choppy flying for most commercial airline operations the past few decades. They've had to contend with wide fluctuations in fuel prices, occasional economic slowdowns, and heightening competition. But through it all, Southwest Airlines just keeps climbing. The Dallas-based carrier has been the most consistent company in the airline industry for many years by taking a totally different approach than the rest of the competition. Southwest is known for offering everyday low fares—with no frills—and frequent flights between its key destinations.

CHAPTER 5

PRESELECTED FOLIOS
FROM FOLIO*FN*

OLIO*fn*.com offers well over 100 preselected Folios for its customers. You can see the whole selection by going to its Web site. Listed here you will find details of 20 preselected Folios, including the stock holdings, the weighting that each stock carries within the portfolio, and the criteria FOLIO*fn* used to select the Folios.

It is important to note, however, that these Folios are subject to change at any time and may have changed by the time you read this. The Folio holdings lists are published here primarily to give you an idea of the types of stocks the Folios feature. For a current list of these and more than 100 other preselected Folios from FOLIO*fn,* please go directly to the Web site.

The Folios listed here include:

1. Folio 30 (Dow Stocks)

2. Global

3. International

4. Folio 50 (50 largest stocks of the S&P 500)

5. Folio OTC (the 50 largest stocks of the Nasdaq 100)

6. Income

7. Large Cap Blend

8. Large Cap Growth

9. Large Cap Value

10. Mid Cap Growth

11. Mid Cap Value

12. Small Cap Growth

13. Small Cap Value

14. Zero Dividend

15. Aggressive

16. Conservative

17. Consumer Staples

18. Energy

19. Environmentally Responsible

20. Socially Responsible Investing—Large Cap

FOLIO 30 FOLIO

How were the stocks in this Folio selected?

All of the stocks contained in the Dow Jones Industrial Average are in the Folio 30.

Here is a summary of some of the steps taken to create this Folio:

1. The 30 stocks in this Folio are the same stocks that were selected by the editors of the *Wall Street Journal* to create the Dow Jones Industrial Average (DJIA).

2. The DJIA is a price-weighted index. That means that each stock's weight in the index is determined by its price per share. The higher the price, the more the stock contributes to the overall index. However, when a customer places an order to buy or sell the Folio 30, the weights are computed using 20-minute delayed stock prices.

How many stocks are in this Folio?

There are 30 stocks in this Folio.

How often are the stocks in this Folio changed?

The stocks in this Folio will change only if the creators of the DJIA decide to change the stocks in the DJIA.

Number	Symbol	Company	Weight (% of Folio)
1	AA	ALCOA INC	2.61%
2	AXP	AMERICAN EXPRESS CO	2.28
3	BA	BOEING CO	2.65
4	C	CITIGROUP INC	3.29
5	CAT	CATERPILLAR INC DEL	3.53
6	DD	DU PONT E I DE NEMOURS & CO	2.93
7	DIS	DISNEY WALT CO DISNEY	1.48
8	EK	EASTMAN KODAK CO	2.16
9	GE	GENERAL ELEC CO	2.66
10	GM	GENERAL MTRS CORP	3.35
11	HD	HOME DEPOT INC	3.51
12	HON	HONEYWELL INTL INC	2.23
13	HWP	HEWLETT PACKARD CO	1.48
14	IBM	INTERNATIONAL BUSINESS MACHS	8.54
15	INTC	INTEL CORP	2.35
16	IP	INTL PAPER CO	2.78
17	JNJ	JOHNSON & JOHNSON	3.97
18	JPM	J P MORGAN CHASE & CO	2.54
19	KO	COCA COLA CO	3.26
20	MCD	MCDONALDS CORP	1.89
21	MMM	MINNESOTA MNG & MFG CO	8.17
22	MO	PHILIP MORRIS COS INC	3.23
23	MRK	MERCK & CO INC	4.10
24	MSFT	MICROSOFT CORP	4.76
25	PG	PROCTER & GAMBLE CO	5.64
26	SBC	SBC COMMUNICATIONS INC	2.75
27	T	AT&T CORP	1.14
28	UTX	UNITED TECHNOLOGIES CORP	4.33
29	WMT	WAL MART STORES INC	3.81
30	XOM	EXXON MOBIL CORP	2.60

GLOBAL FOLIO

How were the stocks in this Folio selected?

Here is a summary of some of the steps taken to create this Folio:

1. We identified five major regions—North America, Latin America, Asia, Europe, and Africa. To determine how many stocks from each region to include, we analyzed the size of that region's stock market value in comparison to the rest of the world. For example, if North America's total market value accounted for 50 percent of the world's total stock market value, then 25 of the 50 stocks are chosen from North America.

2. Based on such calculations, we chose 26 stocks from North America, 1 stock from Latin America, 8 stocks from Asia, 14 stocks from Europe, and 1 stock from Africa.

3. Within each region, the stocks were ranked according to their total stock market value. We chose the stocks with the largest total market values to represent that region.

4. Each stock's proportion is determined by its market capitalization. The higher the market capitalization, the more the stock contributes to the Folio.

How many stocks are in this Folio?

There are 50 stocks in this Folio.

How often are the stocks in this Folio changed?

The Folio is reviewed every year. If the characteristics of the Folio have changed substantially, the stocks included may change. Also, corporate actions, such as a merger, or other events may prompt us to change the stocks at any time.

Number	Symbol	Company	Weight (% of Folio)
1	AIG	AMERICAN INTL GROUP INC	3.05%
2	ALA	ALCATEL ADR	0.54
3	AZN	ASTRAZENECA PLC ADR	1.37
4	BMY	BRISTOL MYERS SQUIBB CO	1.69
5	BP	BP AMOCO P L C ADR	3.20
6	BRK.A	BERKSHIRE HATHAWAY INC DEL CL A	1.65
7	C	CITIGROUP INC	4.23
8	CCL	CARNIVAL CORP	0.27
9	CHL	CHINA MOBILE HONG KONG LTD ADR	1.52
10	CMS	CMS ENERGY CORP	0.06
11	CSCO	CISCO SYS INC	2.57
12	EMC	E M C CORP MASS	1.31
13	ERICY	ERICSSON L M TEL CO ADR CL B SEK10	0.80
14	FTE	FRANCE TELECOM ADR	1.13
15	GE	GENERAL ELEC CO	7.93
16	HBC	HSBC HLDGS PLC ADR NEW	1.17
17	HD	HOME DEPOT INC	1.95
18	HMC	HONDA MOTOR LTD AMERN SHS	0.67
19	IBM	INTERNATIONAL BUSINESS MACHS	3.32
20	ING	ING GROEP N V ADR	1.03
21	INTC	INTEL CORP	3.13
22	JNJ	JOHNSON & JOHNSON	2.17
23	KO	COCA COLA CO	1.92
24	LLY	LILLY ELI & CO	1.51
25	MC	MATSUSHITA ELEC INDL ADR	0.63
26	MO	PHILIP MORRIS COS INC	1.78
27	MRK	MERCK & CO INC	2.67
28	MSFT	MICROSOFT CORP	6.05
29	MTF	MITSUBISHI TOKYO FINL GROUP ADR	0.74
30	NOK	NOKIA CORP ADR	2.37
31	NT	NORTEL NETWORKS LIMITED	0.74
32	NTT	NIPPON TELEG & TEL CORP ADR	1.62
33	ORCL	ORACLE CORP	1.48
34	PFE	PFIZER INC	4.23
35	PG	PROCTER & GAMBLE CO	1.32
36	RD	ROYAL DUTCH PETE CO NY REG GLD1.25	2.08
37	SASOY	SASOL LTD ADR	0.10
38	SBC	SBC COMMUNICATIONS INC	2.29
39	SC	SHELL TRANS & TRADING PLC NEW YRK SH NEW	1.38
40	SNE	SONY CORP ADR NEW	1.21
41	TEF	TELEFONICA S A ADR	1.09

Number	Symbol	Company	Weight (% of Folio)
42	TI	TELECOM ITALIA SPA ADR ORD	0.86%
43	TM	TOYOTA MOTOR CORP SP ADR REP2COM	2.10
44	TSM	TAIWAN SEMICONDUCTOR MFG LTD ADR	0.78
45	V	VIVENDI ADR	1.22
46	VOD	VODAFONE GROUP PLC ADR	2.88
47	VZ	VERIZON COMMUNICATIONS INC.	2.33
48	WFC	WELLS FARGO & CO NEW	1.29
49	WMT	WAL MART STORES INC	3.66
50	XOM	EXXON MOBIL CORP	4.90

INTERNATIONAL FOLIO

How were the stocks in this Folio selected?

Here is a summary of some of the steps taken to create this Folio:

1. We identified four major regions—Latin America, Asia, Europe, and Africa. To determine how many stocks from each region to include, we analyzed the size of that region's stock market value in comparison to the rest of the world. For example, if Asia's total market value accounted for 36 percent of all the regions' total market value, then 18 stocks of the 50 were chosen from Asia.

2. Based on the figures we obtained, we used 1 stock from Latin America, 18 stocks from Asia, 30 stocks from Europe, and 1 stock from Africa.

3. Within each region, the stocks were ranked according to their total stock market value. We chose the stocks with the largest total market values to represent that region.

4. Each stock's proportion is determined by its market capitalization. The higher the market capitalization, the more the stock contributes to the Folio.

How many stocks are in this Folio?

There are 50 stocks in this Folio.

How often are the stocks in this Folio changed?

The Folio is reviewed every year. If the characteristics of the Folio have changed substantially, the stocks included may change. Also, corporate actions, such as a merger, or other events may prompt us to change the stocks at any time.

Number	Symbol	Company	Weight (% of Folio)
1	ABN	ABN AMRO HLDG NV ADR	1.03%
2	AEG	AEGON N V ORD AMER REG	1.37
3	ALA	ALCATEL ADR	1.21
4	AVE	AVENTIS ADR	1.17
5	AXA	AXA ADR	1.78
6	AZN	ASTRAZENECA PLC ADR	3.05
7	BBV	BANCO BILBAO VIZCAYA ARGENTARI ADR	1.54
8	BCS	BARCLAYS PLC ADR	1.87
9	BHP	BHP LTD ADR	0.75
10	BP	BP AMOCO P L C ADR	7.15
11	BTY	BT GROUP PLC ADR	1.51
12	CAJ	CANON INC ADR	1.30
13	CCL	CARNIVAL CORP	0.60
14	CHL	CHINA MOBILE HONG KONG LTD ADR	3.39
15	CWP	CABLE & WIRELESS PUB LTD CO ADR	0.70
16	DEO	DIAGEO P L C ADR NEW	1.30
17	E	ENI S P A ADR	1.84
18	EN	ENEL SOCIETA PER AZIONI ADR	1.46
19	ERICY	ERICSSON L M TEL CO ADR CL B SEK10	1.77
20	FTE	FRANCE TELECOM ADR	2.51
21	FUJIY	FUJI PHOTO FILM LTD ADR	0.76
22	HBC	HSBC HLDGS PLC ADR NEW	2.61
23	HIT	HITACHI LIMITED ADR 10 COM	1.30
24	HMC	HONDA MOTOR LTD AMERN SHS	1.49
25	ING	ING GROEP N V ADR	2.30
26	IYCOY	ITO YOKADO LTD ADR NEW	0.79
27	KTC	KOREA TELECOM ADR	0.56
28	KYO	KYOCERA CORP ADR	0.66
29	MC	MATSUSHITA ELEC INDL ADR	1.40
30	MTF	MITSUBISHI TOKYO FINL GROUP ADR	1.65

Number	Symbol	Company	Weight (% of Folio)
31	NAB	NATIONAL AUSTRALIA BK LTD ADR	0.91%
32	NIPNY	NEC CORP ADR	1.10
33	NOK	NOKIA CORP ADR	5.29
34	NTT	NIPPON TELEG & TEL CORP ADR	3.61
35	PHG	KONINKLIJKE PHILIPS ELECTRS NV ADR NEW	1.39
36	RD	ROYAL DUTCH PETE CO NY REG GLD1.25	4.65
37	SASOY	SASOL LTD ADR	0.23
38	SC	SHELL TRANS & TRADING PLC NEW YRK SH NEW	3.08
39	SKM	SK TELECOM LTD ADR	0.52
40	SNE	SONY CORP ADR NEW	2.71
41	STD	BANCO SANTANDER CENT HISPANO ADR	1.55
42	STM	STMICROELECTRONICS N V	1.28
43	TEF	TELEFONICA S A ADR	2.43
44	TI	TELECOM ITALIA SPA ADR ORD	1.92
45	TM	TOYOTA MOTOR CORP SP ADR REP2COM	4.68
46	TOT	TOTAL FINA S A ADR	1.85
47	TSM	TAIWAN SEMICONDUCTOR MFG LTD ADR	1.74
48	UN	UNILEVER N V N Y SHS NEW	1.11
49	V	VIVENDI ADR	2.71
50	VOD	VODAFONE GROUP PLC ADR	6.42

FOLIO 50

How were the stocks in this Folio selected?

Here is a summary of some of the steps taken to create this Folio:

1. The 500 stocks in the S&P 500 were ranked according to their total stock market value. We selected the 50 stocks with the greatest market values.

2. Each stock's weight is determined by its market capitalization. The higher the market capitalization, the more the stock contributes to the Folio.

How many stocks are in this Folio?

There are 50 stocks in this Folio.

How often are the stocks in this Folio changed?

The Folio is reviewed every quarter. If the characteristics of the Folio have changed substantially, the stocks included may change. Also, corporate actions, such as a merger, or other events may prompt us to change the stocks at any time.

Number	Symbol	Company	Weight (% of Folio)
1	ABT	ABBOTT LABS	1.58%
2	AHP	AMERICAN HOME PRODS CORP	1.47
3	AIG	AMERICAN INTL GROUP INC	3.77
4	AMAT	APPLIED MATLS INC	0.60
5	AMGN	AMGEN INC	1.10
6	AOL	AOL TIME WARNER, INC.	2.49
7	AXP	AMERICAN EXPRESS CO	0.84
8	BAC	BANK OF AMERICA CORPORATION	1.79
9	BLS	BELLSOUTH CORP	1.32
10	BMY	BRISTOL MYERS SQUIBB CO	1.85
11	C	CITIGROUP INC	4.71
12	CMS	CMS ENERGY CORP	0.06
13	CSCO	CISCO SYS INC	2.45
14	CVX	CHEVRONTEXACO CORP	1.74
15	DELL	DELL COMPUTER CORP	1.31
16	DIS	DISNEY WALT CO DISNEY	0.77
17	EMC	E M C CORP MASS	0.54
18	GE	GENERAL ELEC CO	7.34
19	GLW	CORNING INC	0.14
20	HD	HOME DEPOT INC	2.17
21	HWP	HEWLETT PACKARD CO	0.73
22	IBM	INTERNATIONAL BUSINESS MACHS	3.84
23	INTC	INTEL CORP	3.96
24	JNJ	JOHNSON & JOHNSON	3.32
25	JPM	J P MORGAN CHASE & CO	1.30
26	KO	COCA COLA CO	2.15
27	LLY	LILLY ELI & CO	1.61
28	LU	LUCENT TECHNOLOGIES INC	0.38
29	MO	PHILIP MORRIS COS INC	1.82
30	MOT	MOTOROLA INC	0.60

Number	Symbol	Company	Weight (% of Folio)
31	MRK	MERCK & CO INC	2.46%
32	MSFT	MICROSOFT CORP	6.60
33	MWD	MORGAN STANLEY DEAN WITTER&CO NEW	1.10
34	NT	NORTEL NETWORKS LIMITED	0.41
35	ORCL	ORACLE CORP	1.40
36	PEP	PEPSICO INC	1.56
37	PFE	PFIZER INC	4.58
38	PG	PROCTER & GAMBLE CO	1.87
39	RD	ROYAL DUTCH PETE CO NY REG GLD1.25	1.89
40	SBC	SBC COMMUNICATIONS INC	2.41
41	SGP	SCHERING PLOUGH CORP	0.95
42	SUNW	SUN MICROSYSTEMS INC	0.75
43	T	AT&T CORP	1.15
44	TXN	TEXAS INSTRS INC	0.90
45	TYC	TYCO INTL LTD NEW	2.29
46	WCOM	WORLDCOM INC WORLDCOM GROUP	0.77
47	WFC	WELLS FARGO & CO NEW	1.33
48	WMT	WAL MART STORES INC	4.71
49	XOM	EXXON MOBIL CORP	4.91
50	YHOO	YAHOO INC	0.18

FOLIO OTC

How were the stocks in this Folio selected?

Here is a summary of some of the steps taken to create this Folio:

1. The 100 stocks in the Nasdaq 100 were ranked according to their total stock market value. We selected the 50 stocks with the greatest total market values.

2. Each stock's weight is determined by its market capitalization. The higher the market capitalization, the more the stock contributes to the Folio.

How many stocks are in this Folio?

There are 50 stocks in this Folio.

How often are the stocks in this Folio changed?

The Folio is reviewed every quarter. If the characteristics of the Folio have changed substantially, the stocks included may change. Also, corporate actions, such as a merger, or other events may prompt us to change the stocks.

Number	Symbol	Company	Weight (% of Folio)
1	ADCT	ADC TELECOMMUNICATIONS	0.26%
2	ALTR	ALTERA CORP	0.60
3	AMAT	APPLIED MATLS INC	2.31
4	AMCC	APPLIED MICRO CIRCUITS CORP	0.21
5	AMGN	AMGEN INC	3.91
6	BBBY	BED BATH & BEYOND INC	0.64
7	BEAS	BEA SYS INC	0.43
8	BGEN	BIOGEN INC	0.56
9	BMET	BIOMET INC	0.52
10	BRCD	BROCADE COMMUNICATIONS SYS INC	0.56
11	BRCM	BROADCOM CORP CL A	0.27
12	CEFT	CONCORD EFS INC	0.98
13	CHIR	CHIRON CORP	0.55
14	CHKP	CHECK POINT SOFTWARE TECH LTD ORD	0.62
15	CIEN	CIENA CORP	0.31
16	CMCS	COMCAST CORP CL A SPL	2.41
17	CMVT	COMVERSE TECHNOLOGY INC PAR $0.10	0.24
18	COST	COSTCO WHSL CORP NEW	1.27
19	CSCO	CISCO SYS INC	9.49
20	DELL	DELL COMPUTER CORP	4.90
21	EBAY	EBAY INC	1.22
22	FLEX	FLEXTRONICS INTL LTD ORD	0.84
23	GENZ	GENZYME CORP GENL DIV	0.83
24	GMST	GEMSTAR TV GUIDE INTERNATIONAL, INC ORD	0.70
25	IMNX	IMMUNEX CORP NEW	0.93
26	INTC	INTEL CORP	14.90
27	ITWO	I2 TECHNOLOGIES INC	0.18
28	JDSU	JDS UNIPHASE CORP	0.67
29	JNPR	JUNIPER NETWORKS INC	0.44
30	LLTC	LINEAR TECHNOLOGY CORP	0.90
31	MSFT	MICROSOFT CORP	24.24
32	MXIM	MAXIM INTEGRATED PRODS INC	1.23
33	NTAP	NETWORK APPLIANCE INC	0.46
34	NXTL	NEXTEL COMMUNICATIONS INC CL A	0.56

Number	Symbol	Company	Weight (% of Folio)
35	ORCL	ORACLE CORP	5.41%
36	PALM	PALM INC	0.13
37	PAYX	PAYCHEX INC	0.94
38	PMCS	PMC-SIERRA INC	0.25
39	PSFT	PEOPLESOFT INC	0.78
40	QCOM	QUALCOMM INC	2.85
41	SANM	SANMINA CORP	0.48
42	SBUX	STARBUCKS CORP	0.49
43	SEBL	SIEBEL SYS INC	0.76
44	SUNW	SUN MICROSYSTEMS INC	2.67
45	TLAB	TELLABS INC	0.38
46	VRSN	VERISIGN INC	0.56
47	VRTS	VERITAS SOFTWARE CO	1.18
48	VTSS	VITESSE SEMICONDUCTOR CORP	0.17
49	WCOM	WORLDCOM INC WORLDCOM GROUP	2.91
50	XLNX	XILINX INC	0.89

INCOME FOLIO

How were the stocks in this Folio selected?

We selected 30 stocks with the highest dividend yields that also had betas close to 1.0, meaning the stocks rose and fell roughly the same amount as the S&P 500. Here is a summary of some of the steps taken to create this Folio:

1. We ranked all the stocks in the S&P 500 according to their dividend yields.

2. From the list of highest yielding stocks, we selected the 30 that had betas closest to 1.0.

3. The weight of each stock was set so that the Folio has a beta of 1.0.

How many stocks are in this Folio?

There are generally 30 stocks in this Folio.

How often are the stocks in this Folio changed?

The Folio is reviewed every month. If the characteristics of the Folio have changed substantially, the stocks included may change. Also, corporate actions, such as a merger, or other events may prompt us to change the stocks at any time.

Number	Symbol	Company	Weight (% of Folio)
1	AM	AMERICAN GREETINGS CORP CL A	2.00%
2	AOC	AON CORP	2.00
3	ATI	ALLEGHENY TECHNOLOGIES INC	7.50
4	AVP	AVON PRODS INC	2.00
5	BAC	BANK OF AMERICA CORPORATION	3.50
6	BC	BRUNSWICK CORP	2.00
7	CF	CHARTER ONE FINL INC	2.00
8	CTB	COOPER TIRE & RUBR CO	2.00
9	CUM	CUMMINS INC	2.00
10	DCN	DANA CORP	7.50
11	F	FORD MTR CO DEL PAR $0.01	7.50
12	GM	GENERAL MTRS CORP	2.00
13	GR	GOODRICH B F CO	7.50
14	GT	GOODYEAR TIRE & RUBR CO	7.50
15	HON	HONEYWELL INTL INC	2.00
16	IP	INTL PAPER CO	2.00
17	KMG	KERR MCGEE CORP	2.00
18	LPX	LOUISIANA PAC CORP	2.00
19	LTD	LIMITED INC	2.00
20	MEA	MEAD CORP	2.00
21	MRO	USX MARATHON GROUP NEW	2.00
22	R	RYDER SYS INC	2.00
23	ROH	ROHM & HAAS CO	2.00
24	SNA	SNAP ON INC	2.00
25	TRW	TRW INC	7.50
26	UPC	UNION PLANTERS CORP	7.50
27	USB	US BANCORP DEL	2.00
28	WB	WACHOVIA CORP 2ND NEW	2.00
29	WY	WEYERHAEUSER CO	2.00
30	X	USX-U S STL	2.00

LARGE CAP BLEND FOLIO

How were the stocks in this Folio selected?

We selected stocks with a market capitalization greater than $11 billion and the median price-book ratio. Here is a summary of some of the steps taken to create this Folio:

1. We examined all FOLIO*fn* window stocks and identified all large-cap stocks with market capitalizations greater than $11 billion.

2. We ranked these large-cap stocks according to their price-book ratios.

3. We divided the ranked list into thirds.

4. We selected 30 stocks that had price-book ratios in the middle third.

5. We set the weights of these 30 stocks so that the Folio has an average price-book ratio roughly equal to the median price-book ratio of all large-cap blend stocks.

How many stocks are in this Folio?

There are 30 stocks in this Folio.

How often are the stocks in this Folio changed?

The Folio is reviewed every quarter. If the characteristics of the Folio have changed substantially, the stocks included may change. Also, corporate actions, such as a merger, or other events may prompt us to change the stocks at any time.

Number	Symbol	Company	Weight (% of Folio)
1	AOC	AON CORP	2.00%
2	AT	ALLTEL CORP	2.00
3	AVE	AVENTIS ADR	2.00
4	AXP	AMERICAN EXPRESS CO	2.00
5	BBV	BANCO BILBAO VIZCAYA ARGENTARI ADR	2.00

Number	Symbol	Company	Weight (% of Folio)
6	BK	BANK NEW YORK INC	7.50%
7	COST	COSTCO WHSL CORP NEW	2.00
8	CVS	CVS CORP	2.00
9	DNA	GENENTECH INC NEW	7.50
10	DYN	DYNEGY INC	2.00
11	FRE	FEDERAL HOME LN MTG CORP	6.04
12	HI	HOUSEHOLD INTL INC	2.00
13	INTC	INTEL CORP	2.00
14	KRB	MBNA CORP	4.96
15	LOW	LOWES COS INC	7.50
16	LUV	SOUTHWEST AIRLS CO	2.00
17	MCD	MCDONALDS CORP	2.00
18	MEL	MELLON FINL CORP	2.00
19	NKE	NIKE INC CL B	2.00
20	NVS	NOVARTIS A G ADR	7.50
21	SCH	SCHWAB CHARLES CORP NEW	2.00
22	SUNW	SUN MICROSYSTEMS INC	2.00
23	SWY	SAFEWAY INC NEW	2.00
24	TGT	TARGET CORP	7.50
25	TXN	TEXAS INSTRS INC	2.00
26	UL	UNILEVER PLC ADR NEW	2.00
27	USB	US BANCORP DEL	2.00
28	VZ	VERIZON COMMUNICATIONS INC.	7.50
29	WMI	WASTE MGMT INC DEL	2.00
30	XOM	EXXON MOBIL CORP	2.00

LARGE CAP GROWTH FOLIO

How were the stocks in this Folio selected?

We selected stocks with a market capitalization greater than $11 billion and the highest price-book ratio. Here is a summary of some of the steps taken to create this Folio:

1. We examined all FOLIO*fn* window stocks and identified all large-cap stocks, those with market capitalizations greater than $11 billion.

2. We ranked these large-cap stocks according to their price-book ratios.

3. We divided the ranked list into thirds.

4. We selected 30 stocks that had price-book ratios in the highest third.

5. We set the weights of these 30 stocks so that the Folio has an average price-book ratio roughly equal to the median price-book ratio of all large-cap growth stocks.

How many stocks are in this Folio?

There are 30 stocks in this Folio.

How often are the stocks in this Folio changed?

The Folio is reviewed every quarter. If the characteristics of the Folio have changed substantially, the stocks included may change. Also, corporate actions, such as a merger, or other events may prompt us to change the stocks at any time.

Number	Symbol	Company	Weight (% of Folio)
1	AGN	ALLERGAN INC	2.00%
2	AHP	AMERICAN HOME PRODS CORP	2.00
3	AMGN	AMGEN INC	2.19
4	AOL	AOL TIME WARNER, INC.	5.12
5	BMY	BRISTOL MYERS SQUIBB CO	2.00
6	CMVT	COMVERSE TECHNOLOGY INC PAR	2.00
7	EBAY	EBAY INC	2.00
8	EMC	E M C CORP MASS	2.00
9	G	GILLETTE CO	8.77
10	GDT	GUIDANT CORP	2.00
11	GE	GENERAL ELEC CO	2.00
12	HDI	HARLEY DAVIDSON INC	2.00
13	K	KELLOGG CO	2.00
14	KO	COCA COLA CO	2.00
15	KSS	KOHLS CORP	2.00
16	LLTC	LINEAR TECHNOLOGY CORP	2.00
17	LLY	LILLY ELI & CO	2.00
18	MDT	MEDTRONIC INC	2.00
19	MRK	MERCK & CO INC	2.00
20	MXIM	MAXIM INTEGRATED PRODS INC	2.00
21	NOK	NOKIA CORP ADR	3.51

Number	Symbol	Company	Weight (% of Folio)
22	NTAP	NETWORK APPLIANCE INC	14.02%
23	OMC	OMNICOM GROUP INC	2.00
24	PALM	PALM INC	2.00
25	PFE	PFIZER INC	5.39
26	QCOM	QUALCOMM INC	2.00
27	SCH	SCHWAB CHARLES CORP NEW	2.00
28	SEBL	SIEBEL SYS INC	15.00
29	SGP	SCHERING PLOUGH CORP	2.00
30	SLE	SARA LEE CORP	2.00

LARGE CAP VALUE FOLIO

How were the stocks in this Folio selected?

We selected stocks with a market capitalization greater than $11 billion and the lowest price-book ratio. Here is a summary of some of the steps taken to create this Folio:

1. We examined all FOLIO*fn* window stocks and identified all large-cap stocks, those with market capitalizations greater than $11 billion.

2. We ranked these large-cap stocks according to their price-book ratios.

3. We divided the ranked list into thirds.

4. We selected 30 stocks that had price-book ratios in the lowest third.

5. We set the weights of these 30 stocks so that the Folio has an average price-book ratio roughly equal to the median price-book ratio of all large-cap value stocks.

How many stocks are in this Folio?

There are 30 stocks in this Folio.

How often are the stocks in this Folio changed?

The Folio is reviewed every quarter. If the characteristics of the Folio have changed substantially, the stocks included may change. Also, corporate actions, such as a merger, or other events may prompt us to change the stocks at any time.

Number	Symbol	Company	Weight (% of Folio)
1	ABN	ABN AMRO HLDG NV ADR	2.00%
2	BTY	BT GROUP PLC ADR	2.00
3	CA	COMPUTER ASSOC INTL INC	2.00
4	CB	CHUBB CORP	2.00
5	CCL	CARNIVAL CORP	2.00
6	COST	COSTCO WHSL CORP NEW	2.00
7	COX	COX COMMUNICATIONS INC NEW CL A	2.00
8	D	DOMINION RESOURCES INC.	2.00
9	E	ENI S P A ADR	2.00
10	FDX	FEDEX CORP	2.00
11	FON	SPRINT CORP FON GROUP	2.00
12	FPL	FPL GROUP INC	7.20
13	HMC	HONDA MOTOR LTD AMERN SHS	2.00
14	ITWO	I2 TECHNOLOGIES INC	2.00
15	JDSU	JDS UNIPHASE CORP	15.00
16	LEH	LEHMAN BROS HLDGS INC	2.00
17	LMT	LOCKHEED MARTIN CORP	10.80
18	MOT	MOTOROLA INC	2.00
19	MTF	MITSUBISHI TOKYO FINL GROUP ADR	2.00
20	NKE	NIKE INC CL B	2.00
21	NWS	NEWS CORP LTD ADR NEW	2.00
22	ONE	BANK ONE CORP	2.00
23	RD	ROYAL DUTCH PETE CO NY REG GLD1.25	2.00
24	REI	RELIANT ENERGY INC	15.00
25	RTP	RIO TINTO PLC ADR	2.00
26	SO	SOUTHERN CO	2.00
27	STD	BANCO SANTANDER CENT HISPANO ADR	2.00
28	STI	SUNTRUST BKS INC	2.00
29	TI	TELECOM ITALIA SPA ADR ORD	2.00
30	USAI	USA NETWORKS INC	2.00

MID CAP GROWTH FOLIO

How were the stocks in this Folio selected?

We selected stocks with a market capitalization between $1.7 billion and $11 billion and the highest price-book ratio. Here is a summary of some of the steps taken to create this Folio:

1. We examined all FOLIO*fn* window stocks and identified all mid-cap stocks, those with market capitalizations between $1.7 billion and $11 billion.

2. We ranked these mid-cap stocks according to their price-book ratios.

3. We divided the ranked list into thirds.

4. We selected 30 stocks that had price-book ratios in the highest third.

5. We set the weights of these 30 stocks so that the Folio has an average price-book ratio roughly equal to the median price-book ratio of all mid-cap growth stocks.

How many stocks are in this Folio?

There are 30 stocks in this Folio.

How often are the stocks in this Folio changed?

The Folio is reviewed every quarter. If the characteristics of the Folio have changed substantially, the stocks included may change. Also, corporate actions, such as a merger, or other events may prompt us to change the stocks at any time.

Number	Symbol	Company	Weight (% of Folio)
1	ABC	AMERISOURCEBERGEN CORP COM CL A	2.00%
2	ALKS	ALKERMES INC	2.00
3	APOL	APOLLO GROUP INC A	2.96
4	BBBY	BED BATH & BEYOND	2.00

Number	Symbol	Company	Weight (% of Folio)
5	BEC	BECKMAN COULTER	4.93%
6	BGEN	BIOGEN INC	2.00
7	CDWC	CDW COMPUTER CTRS	7.27
8	CEFT	CONCORD EFS INC	2.00
9	CEPH	CEPHALON INC	7.78
10	CSGS	CSG SYS INTL INC	2.00
11	CTXS	CITRIX SYS INC	2.11
12	DCEL	DOBSON COMMUNICATIONS	2.00
13	DJ	DOW JONES & CO INC	2.24
14	DV	DEVRY INC DEL	2.10
15	EMLX	EMULEX CORP NEW	2.13
16	FRX	FOREST LABS INC	2.17
17	ICI	IMPERIAL CHEM INDS PLC ADR NEW	6.67
18	IDPH	IDEC PHARMACEUTICALS	2.25
19	K	KELLOGG CO	5.73
20	MEDI	MEDIMMUNE INC	2.00
21	MIL	MILLIPORE CORP	4.31
22	NVDA	NVIDIA CORP	2.49
23	PMCS	PMC-SIERRA INC	2.00
24	POS	CATALINA MARKETING	2.00
25	PSFT	PEOPLESOFT INC	2.00
26	RHI	ROBERT HALF INTL INC	6.34
27	SYK	STRYKER CORP	5.39
28	TEVA	TEVA PHARMACEUTICAL	2.00
29	TSS	TOTAL SYS SVCS INC	4.59
30	UVN	UNIVISION COMMUNICATIONS INC	4.55

MID CAP VALUE FOLIO

How were the stocks in this Folio selected?

We selected stocks with a market capitalization between $1.7 billion and $11 billion and the lowest price-book ratio. Here is a summary of some of the steps taken to create this Folio:

1. We examined all FOLIO*fn* window stocks and identified all mid-cap stocks, those with market capitalizations between $1.7 billion and $11 billion.

2. We ranked these mid-cap stocks according to their price-book ratios.

3. We divided the ranked list into thirds.

4. We selected 30 stocks that had price-book ratios in the lowest third.

5. We set the weights of these 30 stocks so that the Folio has an average price-book ratio roughly equal to the median price-book ratio of all mid-cap value stocks.

How many stocks are in this Folio?

There are 30 stocks in this Folio.

How often are the stocks in this Folio changed?

The Folio is reviewed every quarter. If the characteristics of the Folio have changed substantially, the stocks included may change. Also, corporate actions, such as a merger, or other events may prompt us to change the stocks at any time.

Number	Symbol	Company	Weight (% of Folio)
1	ABN	ABN AMRO HLDG NV ADR	2.00%
2	BTY	BT GROUP PLC ADR	2.00
3	CA	COMPUTER ASSOC INTL INC	2.00
4	CB	CHUBB CORP	2.00
5	CCL	CARNIVAL CORP	2.00
6	COST	COSTCO WHSL CORP NEW	2.00
7	COX	COX COMMUNICATIONS INC NEW CL A	2.00
8	D	DOMINION RESOURCES INC.	2.00
9	E	ENI S P A ADR	2.00
10	FDX	FEDEX CORP	2.00
11	FON	SPRINT CORP FON GROUP	2.00
12	FPL	FPL GROUP INC	7.20
13	HMC	HONDA MOTOR LTD AMERN SHS	2.00
14	ITWO	I2 TECHNOLOGIES INC	2.00
15	JDSU	JDS UNIPHASE CORP	15.00
16	LEH	LEHMAN BROS HLDGS INC	2.00
17	LMT	LOCKHEED MARTIN CORP	10.80
18	MOT	MOTOROLA INC	2.00

Number	Symbol	Company	Weight (% of Folio)
19	MTF	MITSUBISHI TOKYO FINL GROUP ADR	2.00
20	NKE	NIKE INC CL B	2.00
21	NWS	NEWS CORP LTD ADR NEW	2.00
22	ONE	BANK ONE CORP	2.00
23	RD	ROYAL DUTCH PETE CO NY REG GLD1.25	2.00
24	REI	RELIANT ENERGY INC	15.00
25	RTP	RIO TINTO PLC ADR	2.00
26	SO	SOUTHERN CO	2.00
27	STD	BANCO SANTANDER CENT HISPANO ADR	2.00
28	STI	SUNTRUST BKS INC	2.00
29	TI	TELECOM ITALIA SPA ADR ORD	2.00
30	USAI	USA NETWORKS INC	2.00

SMALL CAP GROWTH FOLIO

How were the stocks in this Folio selected?

We selected stocks with a market capitalization less than $1.7 billion and the highest price-book ratio. Here is a summary of some of the steps taken to create this Folio:

1. We examined all FOLIO*fn* window stocks and identified all small-cap stocks, those with market capitalizations less than $1.7 billion.

2. We ranked these small-cap stocks according to their price-book ratios.

3. We divided the ranked list into thirds.

4. We selected 30 stocks that had price-book ratios in the highest third.

5. We set the weights of these 30 stocks so that the Folio has an average price-book ratio roughly equal to the median price-book ratio of all small-cap growth stocks.

How many stocks are in this Folio?

There are 30 stocks in this Folio.

How often are the stocks in this Folio changed?

The Folio is reviewed every quarter. If the characteristics of the Folio have changed substantially, the stocks included may change. Also, corporate actions, such as a merger, or other events may prompt us to change the stocks at any time.

Number	Symbol	Company	Weight (% of Folio)
1	ACAI	ATLANTIC COAST AIRLINES HLDGS	3.29%
2	AEOS	AMERICAN EAGLE OUTFITTERS NEW	3.37
3	APPB	APPLEBEES INTL INC	3.28
4	CACI	CACI INTL INC CL A	3.34
5	CTIC	CELL THERAPEUTICS INC	3.35
6	DCI	DONALDSON INC	3.30
7	DIGL	DIGITAL LIGHTWAVE INC	3.32
8	DNEX	DIONEX CORP	3.31
9	GB	WILSON GREATBATCH TECHNOLOGIES	3.28
10	GERN	GERON CORP	3.39
11	GGC	GEORGIA GULF CORP PAR $0.01	3.34
12	HAE	HAEMONETICS CORP	3.34
13	HU	HUDSON UNITED BANCORP	3.28
14	ICPT	INTERCEPT GROUP INC	3.37
15	ILOG	ILOG S A ADR	3.35
16	MANH	MANHATTAN ASSOCS INC	3.38
17	MLHR	MILLER HERMAN INC	3.37
18	MME	MID ATLANTIC MED SVCS INC	3.29
19	NATI	NATIONAL INSTRS CORP	3.36
20	OFIX	ORTHOFIX INTL N V	3.37
21	OO	OAKLEY INC	3.29
22	PAA	PLAINS ALL AMERN PIPELINE L P UNIT LTD P	3.32
23	PLB	AMERICAN ITALIAN PASTA CO CL A	3.30
24	PLXS	PLEXUS CORP	3.35
25	PXLW	PIXELWORKS INC	3.38
26	RMBS	RAMBUS INC DEL	3.35
27	ROP	ROPER INDS INC NEW	3.32
28	SMMX	SYMYX TECHNOLOGIES	3.38
29	SONO	SONOSITE INC	3.36
30	VGIN	VISIBLE GENETICS INC	3.27

SMALL CAP VALUE FOLIO

How were the stocks in this Folio selected?

We selected stocks with a market capitalization less than $1.7 billion and the lowest price-book ratio. Here is a summary of some of the steps taken to create this Folio:

1. We examined all FOLIO*fn* window stocks and identified all small-cap stocks, those with market capitalizations less than $1.7 billion.

2. We ranked these small-cap stocks according to their price-book ratios.

3. We divided the ranked list into thirds.

4. We selected 30 stocks that had price-book ratios in the lowest third.

5. We set the weights of these 30 stocks so that the Folio has an average price-book ratio roughly equal to the median price-book ratio of all small-cap value stocks.

How many stocks are in this Folio?

There are 30 stocks in this Folio.

How often are the stocks in this Folio changed?

The Folio is reviewed every quarter. If the characteristics of the Folio have changed substantially, the stocks included may change. Also, corporate actions, such as a merger, or other events may prompt us to change the stocks at any time.

Number	Symbol	Company	Weight (% of Folio)
1	ACAI	ATLANTIC COAST AIRLINES HLDGS	3.29%
2	AEOS	AMERICAN EAGLE OUTFITTERS NEW	3.37
3	APPB	APPLEBEES INTL INC	3.28
4	CACI	CACI INTL INC CL A	3.34

Number	Symbol	Company	Weight (% of Folio)
5	CTIC	CELL THERAPEUTICS INC	3.35%
6	DCI	DONALDSON INC	3.30
7	DIGL	DIGITAL LIGHTWAVE INC	3.32
8	DNEX	DIONEX CORP	3.31
9	GB	WILSON GREATBATCH TECHNOLOGIES	3.28
10	GERN	GERON CORP	3.39
11	GGC	GEORGIA GULF CORP PAR $0.01	3.34
12	HAE	HAEMONETICS CORP	3.34
13	HU	HUDSON UNITED BANCORP	3.28
14	ICPT	INTERCEPT GROUP INC	3.37
15	ILOG	ILOG S A ADR	3.35
16	MANH	MANHATTAN ASSOCS INC	3.38
17	MLHR	MILLER HERMAN INC	3.37
18	MME	MID ATLANTIC MED SVCS INC	3.29
19	NATI	NATIONAL INSTRS CORP	3.36
20	OFIX	ORTHOFIX INTL N V	3.37
21	OO	OAKLEY INC	3.29
22	PAA	PLAINS ALL AMERN PIPELINE L P UNIT LTD P	3.32
23	PLB	AMERICAN ITALIAN PASTA CO CL A	3.30
24	PLXS	PLEXUS CORP	3.35
25	PXLW	PIXELWORKS INC	3.38
26	RMBS	RAMBUS INC DEL	3.35
27	ROP	ROPER INDS INC NEW	3.32
28	SMMX	SYMYX TECHNOLOGIES	3.38
29	SONO	SONOSITE INC	3.36
30	VGIN	VISIBLE GENETICS INC	3.27

ZERO DIVIDEND FOLIO

How were the stocks in this Folio selected?

Here is a summary of some of the steps taken to create this Folio:

1. We created a list of S&P 500 stocks that did not pay dividends in the past year.

2. From this group, we selected the 30 stocks that had betas closest to 1.0.

3. The weight of each stock was set so that the Folio has a beta of 1.0.

How many stocks are in this Folio?

There may be between 20 and 30 stocks in this Folio.

How often are the stocks in this Folio changed?

The Folio is reviewed every month. If the characteristics of the Folio have changed substantially, the stocks included may change. Also, corporate actions, such as a merger, or other events may prompt us to change the stocks at any time.

Number	Symbol	Company	Weight (% of Folio)
1	AMGN	AMGEN INC	2.96%
2	BGEN	BIOGEN INC	3.00
3	CCU	CLEAR CHANNEL COMMUNICATIONS	3.55
4	CHIR	CHIRON CORP	2.96
5	CMCSK	COMCAST CORP CL A SPL	2.94
6	CSC	COMPUTER SCIENCES CORP	3.33
7	CVG	CONVERGYS CORP	3.41
8	FCX	FREEPORT-MCMORAN COPPER & GOLD CL B	3.18
9	FD	FEDERATED DEPT STORES INC DEL	3.15
10	FDX	FEDEX CORP	3.09
11	FMC	F M C CORP NEW	3.02
12	HCR	MANOR CARE INC NEW	3.68
13	HUM	HUMANA INC	3.46
14	KM	K MART CORP	3.48
15	KSS	KOHLS CORP	3.18
16	LXK	LEXMARK INTERNATIONAL, INC CL A	3.54
17	MDR	MCDERMOTT INTL INC	3.09
18	MEDI	MEDIMMUNE INC	3.65
19	N	INCO LTD	3.74
20	NCR	NCR CORP NEW	3.50
21	NSM	NATIONAL SEMICONDUCTOR CORP	3.20
22	ODP	OFFICE DEPOT INC	3.44
23	SBUX	STARBUCKS CORP	3.68
24	SPLS	STAPLES INC	3.43
25	TMO	THERMO ELECTRON CORP	3.18

Number	Symbol	Company	Weight (% of Folio)
26	TNB	THOMAS & BETTS CORP	3.30%
27	TSG	SABRE HLDGS CORP CL A	3.31
28	U	US AIRWAYS GROUP INC	3.76
29	UIS	UNISYS CORP	3.33
30	UVN	UNIVISION COMMUNICATIONS INC CL A	3.43

AGGRESSIVE FOLIO

How were the stocks in this Folio selected?

Here is a summary of some of the steps taken to create this Folio:

1. The average market capitalization and price-book ratio were calculated for the stocks included in the S&P 500.

2. We selected the 30 stocks that had betas closest to 1.4 and market capitalizations and price-book ratios closest to the S&P 500 average.

3. The weight of each stock was set so that the Folio's characteristics are as close as possible to the S&P 500 and the desired beta.

How many stocks are in this Folio?

There may be between 20 and 30 stocks in this Folio.

How often are the stocks in this Folio changed?

The Folio is reviewed every month. If the characteristics of the Folio have changed substantially, the stocks included may change. Also, corporate actions, such as a merger, or other events may prompt us to change the stocks at any time.

Number	Symbol	Company	Weight (% of Folio)
1	AL	ALCAN INC COM	7.50%
2	AOC	AON CORP	2.00
3	BDK	BLACK & DECKER CORP	5.70
4	BEN	FRANKLIN RES INC	2.00
5	BK	BANK NEW YORK INC	2.00
6	CA	COMPUTER ASSOC INTL INC	2.00
7	CL	COLGATE PALMOLIVE CO	2.00
8	CMVT	COMVERSE TECHNOLOGY INC PAR $0.10	7.50
9	COST	COSTCO WHSL CORP NEW	2.00
10	EMC	E M C CORP MASS	2.00
11	ETS	ENTERASYS NETWORKS INC	2.00
12	FBF	FLEETBOSTON FINL CORP	2.00
13	GR	GOODRICH B F CO	7.50
14	HIG	HARTFORD FINL SVCS GROUP INC	2.00
15	JPM	J P MORGAN CHASE & CO	2.00
16	LIZ	LIZ CLAIBORNE INC	7.50
17	MMC	MARSH & MCLENNAN COS INC	2.00
18	MOLX	MOLEX INC	2.00
19	NT	NORTEL NETWORKS LIMITED	2.00
20	ODP	OFFICE DEPOT INC	7.50
21	PGR	PROGRESSIVE CORP OHIO	2.00
22	RDC	ROWAN COS INC	7.50
23	RIG	TRANSOCEAN SEDCO FOREX INC ORD	2.00
24	SAPE	SAPIENT CORP	5.30
25	SUNW	SUN MICROSYSTEMS INC	2.00
26	TGT	TARGET CORP	2.00
27	UNH	UNITEDHEALTH GROUP	2.00
28	UTX	UNITED TECHNOLOGIES CORP	2.00
29	VRTS	VERITAS SOFTWARE CO	2.00
30	XLNX	XILINX INC	2.00

CONSERVATIVE FOLIO

How were the stocks in this Folio selected?

Here is a summary of some of the steps taken to create this Folio:

1. The average market capitalization and price-book ratio were calculated for the stocks included in the S&P 500.

2. We selected the 30 stocks that had betas closest to 0.6 and market capitalizations and price-book ratios closest to the S&P 500 average.

3. The weight of each stock was set so that the Folio's characteristics are as close as possible to the S&P 500 and the desired beta.

How many stocks are in this Folio?

There may be between 20 and 30 stocks in this Folio.

How often are the stocks in this Folio changed?

The Folio is reviewed every month. If the characteristics of the Folio have changed substantially, the stocks included may change. Also, corporate actions, such as a merger, or other events may prompt us to change the stocks at any time.

Number	Symbol	Company	Weight (% of Folio)
1	ABK	AMBAC FINL GROUP INC	3.00%
2	APD	AIR PRODS & CHEMS INC	5.23
3	ASO	AMSOUTH BANCORPORATION	3.22
4	BR	BURLINGTON RES INC	2.03
5	BSX	BOSTON SCIENTIFIC CORP	7.50
6	CAG	CONAGRA INC	4.82
7	CBE	COOPER INDS INC	3.33
8	CMA	COMERICA INC	2.06
9	DE	DEERE & CO	2.06
10	DOV	DOVER CORP	4.24
11	DPH	DELPHI AUTOMOTIVE SYS CORP	2.00
12	DVN	DEVON ENERGY CORP NEW	2.00
13	FO	FORTUNE BRANDS INC	4.59
14	HRC	HEALTHSOUTH CORP	2.00
15	JCI	JOHNSON CTLS INC	2.76
16	JP	JEFFERSON PILOT CORP	2.34
17	MAR	MARRIOTT INTL INC NEW CL A	3.10
18	MAY	MAY DEPT STORES CO	2.79
19	MBI	MBIA INC	2.00
20	MTG	MGIC INVT CORP WIS	4.50
21	NWL	NEWELL RUBBERMAID INC	3.69
22	OXY	OCCIDENTAL PETE CORP DEL	2.00
23	PPG	PPG INDS INC	3.26

Number	Symbol	Company	Weight (% of Folio)
24	RGBK	REGIONS FINL CORP	2.00%
25	SOTR	SOUTHTRUST CORP	2.27
26	TMK	TORCHMARK CORP	3.17
27	TXT	TEXTRON INC	2.00
28	UCL	UNOCAL CORP	5.96
29	WLL	WILLAMETTE INDS INC	2.60
30	WLP	WELLPOINT HEALTH NETWORK NEW	7.50

CONSUMER STAPLES FOLIO

How were the stocks in this Folio selected?

Here is a summary of some of the steps taken to create this Folio:

1. We created a list of all stocks in the consumer staples sector as defined by Zacks Consumer Staples sector that are FOLIO*fn* window stocks.

2. We ranked the stocks according to market capitalization (total stock market value) and chose the 30 stocks with the highest market capitalizations.

3. We equally weighted all stocks in the Folio, meaning that each stock's weight of the Folio is the same.

How many stocks are in this Folio?

There may be between 20 and 30 stocks in this Folio. There may be less if we do not have enough stocks in that sector among our window stocks.

How often are the stocks in this Folio changed?

The Folio is reviewed every quarter. If the characteristics of the Folio have changed substantially, the stocks included may change. Also, corporate actions, such as a merger, or other events may prompt us to change the stocks at any time.

Number	Symbol	Company	Weight (% of Folio)
1	BTI	BRITISH AMERN TOB PLC ADR	3.33%
2	BUD	ANHEUSER BUSCH COS INC	3.33
3	CAG	CONAGRA INC	3.33
4	CCE	COCA COLA ENTERPRISES INC	3.33
5	CL	COLGATE PALMOLIVE CO	3.33
6	CLX	CLOROX CO DEL	3.33
7	CPB	CAMPBELL SOUP CO	3.33
8	CSG	CADBURY SCHWEPPES PLC ADR	3.33
9	DA	GROUPE DANONE ADR	3.33
10	DEO	DIAGEO P L C ADR NEW	3.33
11	EL	LAUDER ESTEE COS INC CL A	3.33
12	G	GILLETTE CO	3.33
13	GCI	GANNETT INC	3.33
14	HNZ	HEINZ H J CO	3.33
15	K	KELLOGG CO	3.33
16	KFT	KRAFT FOODS INC	3.33
17	KMB	KIMBERLY CLARK CORP	3.33
18	KO	COCA COLA CO	3.33
19	LVMHY	LVMH MOET HENNESSY LOU VUITTON ADR	3.33
20	MHP	MCGRAW HILL COS INC	3.33
21	MO	PHILIP MORRIS COS INC	3.33
22	NKE	NIKE INC CL B	3.33
23	NWS	NEWS CORP LTD ADR NEW	3.33
24	PEP	PEPSICO INC	3.33
25	PG	PROCTER & GAMBLE CO	3.33
26	RUK	REED INTL PLC ADR NEW	3.33
27	SLE	SARA LEE CORP	3.33
28	TRB	TRIBUNE CO NEW	3.33
29	UL	UNILEVER PLC ADR NEW	3.33
30	UN	UNILEVER N V N Y SHS NEW	3.33

ENERGY FOLIO

How were the stocks in this Folio selected?

Here is a summary of some of the steps taken to create this Folio:

1. We created a list of all stocks in the energy sector as defined by Zacks Oils and Energy sector that are FOLIO*fn* window stocks.

2. We ranked the stocks according to market capitalization (total stock market value) and chose the 30 stocks with the highest market capitalizations.

3. We equally weighted all stocks in the Folio, meaning that each stock's weight of the Folio is the same.

How many stocks are in this Folio?

There may be between 20 and 30 stocks in this Folio. There may be less if we do not have enough stocks in that sector among our window stocks.

How often are the stocks in this Folio changed?

The Folio is reviewed every quarter. If the characteristics of the Folio have changed substantially, the stocks included may change. Also, corporate actions, such as a merger, or other events may prompt us to change the stocks at any time.

Number	Symbol	Company	Weight (% of Folio)
1	APC	ANADARKO PETE CORP	3.33%
2	BHI	BAKER HUGHES INC	3.33
3	BHP	BHP LTD ADR	3.33
4	BP	BP AMOCO P L C ADR	3.33
5	BR	BURLINGTON RES INC	3.33
6	BRG	BG PLC ADR FIN INST N	3.33
7	COC	CONOCO INC	3.33
8	CVX	CHEVRONTEXACO CORP	3.33
9	DYN	DYNEGY INC	3.33
10	E	ENI S P A ADR	3.33
11	EPG	EL PASO CORP	3.33
12	HAL	HALLIBURTON CO	3.33
13	IMO	IMPERIAL OIL LTD NEW	3.33
14	KMI	KINDER MORGAN INC KANS	3.33
15	MRO	USX MARATHON GROUP NEW	3.33
16	OXY	OCCIDENTAL PETE CORP DEL	3.33
17	P	PHILLIPS PETE CO	3.33
18	PTR	PETROCHINA CO LTD ADR	3.33
19	RD	ROYAL DUTCH PETE CO NY REG GLD1.25	3.33

Number	Symbol	Company	Weight (% of Folio)
20	REP	REPSOL YPF S A ADR	3.33%
21	RIG	TRANSOCEAN SEDCO FOREX INC ORD	3.33
22	SC	SHELL TRANS & TRADING PLC NEW YRK SH NEW	3.33
23	SLB	SCHLUMBERGER LTD	3.33
24	SNP	CHINA PETE & CHEM CORP ADR H SHS	3.33
25	TOT	TOTAL FINA S A ADR	3.33
26	UCL	UNOCAL CORP	3.33
27	WFT	WEATHERFORD INTL INC	3.33
28	WMB	WILLIAMS COS INC DEL	3.33
29	XOM	EXXON MOBIL CORP	3.33
30	YPF	YPF SOCIEDAD ANONIMA ADR CL D	3.33

ENVIRONMENTALLY RESPONSIBLE FOLIO

How were the stocks in this Folio selected?

Here is a summary of some of the steps taken to create this Folio:

1. The stocks in the Investor Responsibility Research Center's database were sorted according to stocks that have no toxic emissions, oil and chemical spills, or compliance penalties, and have not recently been identified as a potentially responsible party for superfund sites by the EPA.

2. Of those, the 30 largest stocks by market capitalization from our window stocks were selected.

3. We equally weighted all stocks in the Folio, meaning that the amount of each stock is the same.

How many stocks are in this Folio?

There are 30 stocks in this Folio.

How often are the stocks in this Folio changed?

The Folio is reviewed every month. If the characteristics of the Folio have changed substantially, the stocks included may change. Also, corporate actions, such as a merger, or other events may prompt us to change the stocks at any time.

Number	Symbol	Company	Weight (% of Folio)
1	AIG	AMERICAN INTL GROUP INC	3.33%
2	AMGN	AMGEN INC	3.33
3	AXP	AMERICAN EXPRESS CO	3.33
4	BAC	BANK OF AMERICA CORPORATION	3.33
5	BK	BANK NEW YORK INC	3.33
6	CA	COMPUTER ASSOC INTL INC	3.33
7	CCU	CLEAR CHANNEL COMMUNICATIONS	3.33
8	CMCSK	COMCAST CORP CL A SPL	3.33
9	CSCO	CISCO SYS INC	3.33
10	DELL	DELL COMPUTER CORP	3.33
11	EDS	ELECTRONIC DATA SYS NEW	3.33
12	FBF	FLEETBOSTON FINL CORP	3.33
13	FNM	FEDERAL NATL MTG ASSN	3.33
14	FON	SPRINT CORP FON GROUP	3.33
15	FRE	FEDERAL HOME LN MTG CORP	3.33
16	GPS	GAP INC DEL	3.33
17	HD	HOME DEPOT INC	3.33
18	JPM	J P MORGAN CHASE & CO	3.33
19	MMC	MARSH & MCLENNAN COS INC	3.33
20	MSFT	MICROSOFT CORP	3.33
21	MWD	MORGAN STANLEY DEAN WITTER& CO NEW	3.33
22	NXTL	NEXTEL COMMUNICATIONS INC CL A	3.33
23	ONE	BANK ONE CORP	3.33
4	ORCL	ORACLE CORP	3.33
25	PCS	SPRINT CORP PCS COM SER 1	3.33
26	QCOM	QUALCOMM INC	3.33
27	SUNW	SUN MICROSYSTEMS INC	3.34
28	USB	US BANCORP DEL	3.33
29	WCOM	WORLDCOM INC WORLDCOM GROUP	3.33
30	WFC	WELLS FARGO & CO NEW	3.33

SOCIALLY RESPONSIBLE INVESTING— LARGE CAP FOLIO

How were the stocks in this Folio selected?

Here is a summary of some of the steps taken to create this Folio:

1. The stocks in the Investor Responsibility Research Center's database were sorted according to stocks that do not derive any revenue from the manufacturing of tobacco, firearms, military weapons, or alcohol, or from the operation of gambling establishments.

2. Of those, the 30 largest stocks by market capitalization from our window stocks were selected.

3. We equally weighted all stocks in the Folio, meaning each stock's weight of the Folio is the same.

How many stocks are in this Folio?

There are 30 stocks in this Folio.

How often are the stocks in this Folio changed?

The Folio is reviewed every month. If the characteristics of the Folio have changed substantially, the stocks included may change. Also, corporate actions, such as a merger, or other events may prompt us to change the stocks at any time.

Number	Symbol	Company	Weight (% of Folio)
1	AMGN	AMGEN INC	3.33%
2	AXP	AMERICAN EXPRESS CO	3.33
3	BAC	BANK OF AMERICA CORPORATION	3.33
4	BLS	BELLSOUTH CORP	3.33
5	BRCM	BROADCOM CORP CL A	3.33
6	CMCSK	COMCAST CORP CL A SPL	3.34
7	CSCO	CISCO SYS INC	3.33
8	F	FORD MTR CO DEL PAR $0.01	3.33
9	FBF	FLEETBOSTON FINL CORP	3.33

Number	Symbol	Company	Weight (% of Folio)
10	FITB	FIFTH THIRD BANCORP	3.33%
11	FNM	FEDERAL NATL MTG ASSN	3.33
12	FRE	FEDERAL HOME LN MTG CORP	3.33
13	HD	HOME DEPOT INC	3.33
14	HI	HOUSEHOLD INTL INC	3.33
15	JPM	J P MORGAN CHASE & CO	3.33
16	KRB	MBNA CORP	3.33
17	MMC	MARSH & MCLENNAN COS INC	3.33
18	MSFT	MICROSOFT CORP	3.33
19	MWD	MORGAN STANLEY DEAN WITTER& CO NEW	3.33
20	NXTL	NEXTEL COMMUNICATIONS INC CL A	3.33
21	ONE	BANK ONE CORP	3.33
22	PCS	SPRINT CORP PCS COM SER 1	3.33
23	SEBL	SIEBEL SYS INC	3.33
24	SLR	SOLECTRON CORP	3.33
25	SUNW	SUN MICROSYSTEMS INC	3.33
26	USB	US BANCORP DEL	3.33
27	WCOM	WORLDCOM INC WORLDCOM GROUP	3.33
28	WFC	WELLS FARGO & CO NEW	3.33
29	XLNX	XILINX INC	3.33
30	YHOO	YAHOO INC	3.33

INDEX

FREE FOLIO FOLLOW-UP AT ALLSTARSTOCKS.COM

Learn more on building your own Folio of all-star stocks and take advantage of a broad range of investment research and links to valuable investment tools at <www.allstarstocks.com>.

AllstarStocks.com, which is operated by author Gene Walden, is currently free, and includes articles, research on stocks and mutual funds, and a series of preselected all-star stock Folios you can use to begin building your own diverse portfolio.

SHARE THE PHENOMENON!

FOR SPECIAL DISCOUNTS on 20 or more copies of *The Folio Phenomenon: New Freedom to Customize Your Investments and Increase Your Wealth,* contact Robin Bermel in Special Sales at 800-621-9621, extension 4455, or by e-mail at bermel@dearborn.com.

Your company also can order this book with a customized cover featuring your name, logo, and message.